W9-BTT-468

Jim **Burke**

tools&texts

for

50 **essential** *lessons*

Grades 9–12

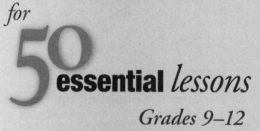

HEINEMANN • PORTSMOUTH, NH

*first*hand
HEINEMANN

*first*hand
An imprint of Heinemann
A division of Reed Elsevier Inc.
361 Hanover Street
Portsmouth, NH 03801–3912
www.firsthand.heinemann.com

Offices and agents throughout the world

Library of Congress Cataloging-in-Publications Data
CIP data is on file with the Library of Congress

ISBN 0-325-01108-7 (Lesson book)
     0-325-01109-5 (Tools and Texts)
     0-325-00857-4 (set)

Printed in the United States of America on acid-free paper

10 09 08 07 06   ML   1 2 3 4 5 6

TABLE OF CONTENTS

Tools

Texts

LESSON PLANNING TEMPLATE

Class: _____ Period: _____ Date: _____

Lesson: _____

PLANNING
▶ **Frame the Lesson:** *position the lesson within your curriculum and your students' academic needs.*
▶ **Essential Skill Set:** *list specific instructional activities.*
▶ **Gather and Prepare:** *list the resources you'll need and suggestions for adapting the lesson for your students.*

TEACHING
▶ **Teach:**
- *develop instructional language, moves, and prompts*
- *subdivide the lesson*
- *identify discussion topics*
- *provide tangible and concrete examples*

ASSESSING
▶ **Assess and Extend:**
- *list strategies to provide extra support or extra challenge*
- *assess understanding of lesson*
- *reinforce and extend lesson*

▷ **Frame the Lesson** _____

▷ **Essential Skill Set** _____

▷ **Gather and Prepare** _____

◀ **Teach** _____

▷ **Assess and Extend** _____

Notes:

Name: _____ Period: _____ Date: _____

Academic Habits Self-Evaluation

DIRECTIONS

Assess yourself in each class using this scale: 1=Always   2=Usually   3=Sometimes   4=Rarely   5=Never

Academic Habits	1	2	3	4	5	6	7	TOTAL
1. I ask for help if I do not understand something.								
2. I bring all the necessary supplies.								
3. I bring my textbook.								
4. I check my work before I turn it in to make sure it satisfies all the requirements and is my "best work."								
5. I come to class on time.								
6. I complete all homework.								
7. I have a dedicated place where I do my homework.								
8. I keep my student ID card with me at all times.								
9. I keep old assignments, quizzes, and tests until the semester ends (to review and to prove my grades).								
10. I keep track of my standing in each class.								
11. I listen to what the teacher and other students say.								
12. I organize all notes and materials in a binder with section dividers that are labeled.								
13. I participate in full class discussions.								
14. I participate in small-group discussions.								
15. I read all the directions before taking tests or doing assignments.								
16. I review my tests/assignments after I get them back.								
17. I set aside specific time for doing homework.								
18. I set goals and make plans to help me achieve them.								
19. I study before all quizzes and exams.								
20. I take notes during lectures, discussions, or videos.								
21. I take notes when I read the assigned readings.								
22. I use a planner to keep track of events/assignments.								
23. I use specific strategies and aids to understand and remember information.								
24. I use specific strategies to help me do my work well and focus my attention.								
25. I write down the homework assignments.								
Grand Total								
Estimated (current) letter grade in this class								

1. In _____ (favorite/strongest class), my teacher would say I am:

1. _____   2. _____   3. _____

2. In _____ (least favorite/hardest class), my teacher would say I am:

1. _____   2. _____   3. _____

3. Reflective Essay

Using the information (your scores) and words from above, write a 1–2 page reflection on the type of student you are and would like to be. Discuss those things you do well and those areas you need to improve to become an even better student. Be sure to provide examples and discuss them as they relate to the ideas in your paper.

▶ Academic Writing

FOCUS

Subject
What you are writing about
(e.g., Hamlet, the Depression,
modern art)

Main Idea
What you are trying to say about
the subject. This is also known as
your "point," as in
"What's your *point*?"

ORGANIZATION

Cause-Effect
Arranged to show connections
between a result and the events
that preceded it.
Also known as
Problem-Solution.

Classification
Organized into categories or
groups according to various
traits.

Comparison-Contrast
Organized to emphasize similari-
ties and differences.

Listing
Arranged in a list with no consid-
eration for other qualities.

Mixed
Organized using a blend of patterns. Might, for example, classify
groups while also comparing or
contrasting them.

Order of Degree
Organized in order of importance, value, or some other
quality.
Also known as **Order
of Importance.**

Sequential
Arranged in the order that events
occur.
Also known as **Time** order or
Chronological order.

Spatial
Arranged according to location or
geographical order.
Also known as **Geographical**
order.

DEVELOPMENT

Examples
Primary text
Secondary texts
Class discussions
Outside world

Details
Sensory
Background
Factual

Quotations
Direct
Indirect
Primary text
Secondary texts

Explanations
Importance
Meaning
Purpose
Effect

Elaborations
Connections
Clarifications
Comparisons
Contrasts
Consequences
Concessions

PURPOSE

Cause and Effect
Answers the question,
"Why did it happen?"

Classification
Answers the questions,
"What kind is it?" or
"What are its parts?"

Compare-Contrast
Answers the questions,
"What is it like?" or
"How is it different?"

Definition
Answers the question,
"What is it?"

Description
Answers the question,
"What does it look, sound, smell,
taste, or feel like?"

Illustration
Answers the question,
"What is an example?"

Narration
Answers the question,
"What happened and when?"

Persuasion
Answers the question,
"Why should I want to do, think,
or value that?"

Problem-Solution
Answers the question,
"What is the problem and how
can it be solved?"

Process Analysis
Answers the question,
"How did it happen?"

© 2007 by Jim Burke from *50 Essential Lessons* (Portsmouth, NH: Heinemann). This page may be reproduced for classroom use only.

Name: _____ Period: _____ Date: _____

◗ ACCESS Final Exam

___DIRECTIONS___ You have two hours to complete both portions of the final exam. What time remains is yours to study for other finals. Such studying must be silent to ensure others have a proper environment in which to take the test and write their essay. Thank you for your hard work and the respect you show your classmates during the final today.

Part 1 *Scholastic Reading Inventory*

This formal reading assessment measures your reading progress this semester. It should take about an hour; you have as much time as you need to complete it. It is more important that you do your very best on Part 1 than Part 2; in other words, do not feel you should rush at all to complete Part 1.

Part 2 Essay: The Elements of Success: Reflecting on the Past and Next Semester

This semester we have heard nearly a dozen speakers from different fields of expertise. Many of them struggled to find out what they wanted to do; success did not come immediately to most of them. Over the semester we have listened to these speakers and read articles about other people. We have tried to identify the "Elements of Success" so that we might apply these elements to our own lives and achieve success in school, at home, and in the future as adults.

In a 2-3 page essay, identify what you feel are the most important elements of success. You may refer to the "Elements of Success" chart we created on the front wall. In your essay, you should:

- Identify the most important elements (plural) of success in school, work, and one's personal life.
- Discuss these elements in your introduction (first paragraph).
- Write a paragraph about each separate element. In *each* paragraph:
  - Explain how this element contributes to success.
  - Provide examples from articles we have read, speakers we have heard, or your own personal experience this year.
  - Explain how each example relates to your point about success.
  - Discuss how this element of success *contributed to your success* in and outside of school. For example, if you say "take risks" is one of the elements of success, discuss the risks you took and how they led to your success; or, if you have not been successful, discuss why you did not take risks.
- Conclude your essay with a final paragraph (or two, if necessary) in which you reflect on your successes and failures this semester and how you can use the lessons of this semester to achieve greater success next semester.

Name: _____ Period: _____ Date: _____

▶ Active Reading: Questions to Consider and Use

QUESTIONS	ACTIONS
▶ BEFORE	
1. What do I think this text will be about? (*Why* do I think that?)	Make predictions
2. What do I know about this subject, text, or author?	Generate connections
3. Why am I reading this text? (What is my guiding question?)	Set/Identify purpose
4. What do I need to be able to do when I finish reading it?	Make a plan
5. What type of text is this? (if a poem, what genre? e.g., a sonnet?)	Preview the text
6. What do I need to know about this type of text to read it?	Evaluate details for importance
7. What is the subject of the text?	Identify the subject
8. What do I know about this subject?	Access background knowledge
9. How does this text connect to what we've studied, read, or done?	Make connections
10. What strategy, technique, or tool(s) should I use to read this?	Make a plan/Use a method
▶ DURING	
11. What do I notice about the text?	Evaluate importance
12. What is the author saying about the subject?	Understand the main idea
13. What don't I understand? (*Why* don't I understand this part?)	Monitor performance
14. How is the information organized within the text?	Analyze organizational patterns
15. Which reading strategies or techniques are working most effectively?	Evaluate methods
16. What *other* possible interpretations/readings are there?	Generate possibilities
17. What feelings does this text inspire in me? (Why? How?)	Connect: Personal
18. How does this text connect with other people, ideas, or texts?	Connect: Comparison
19. What questions would I ask the author or a character at this point?	Use questions to clarify and connect
20. What are some key images or sensory details in what I just read?	Visualize the text
21. What are the most important events, moments, changes?	Evaluate importance
22. How would I answer my guiding question (#3) now?	Monitor progress toward purpose
23. What has changed as I have read on? Why? In what ways?	Read with a purpose
24. What generalizations can I make about the text or author so far? How?	Make inferences/Draw conclusions
25. Are my inferences, predictions, and interpretations accurate?	Monitor accuracy and clarity
26. How ready am I to write about, discuss, or take a test on this text?	Evaluate progress toward goal(s)
27. What challenges does the author face in this text?	Examine craft
28. Is the text accurate? Reliable? Credible? Consistent?	Evaluate ethos
29. How else might the author explain/represent this info or idea?	Generate possibilities
30. How well do I understand what I have read?	Monitor performance
▶ AFTER	
31. What was the author trying to achieve? (Did the author succeed?)	Evaluate purpose/performance
32. What was the author's main idea about the subject?	Pause and reflect
33. Of the techniques and strategies I used, which worked best? Why?	Evaluate process and performance
34. What do I still not understand?	Evaluate comprehension
35. What are some other possible interpretations of this text?	Generate possibilities
36. What details or aspects of the text matter most? Why?	Evaluate textual features
37. What is the most important word, phrase, event, idea, or person?	Evaluate importance
38. What other texts, authors, or ideas might I compare this to?	Make connections
39. Did I read and interpret the text differently than others? How?	Compare performances and processes
40. What caused me the most trouble? Why? (How did I resolve it?)	Pause and reflect
41. What do I need to be sure to remember after reading this?	Pause and reflect
42. How will I ensure that I remember what is important?	Remember
43. When rereading, what should I focus on or try to accomplish?	(Re)Read with a purpose
44. How does this text connect with my own ideas, experiences, values?	Connect: Personal
45. What in the text changed from the beginning to the end? Explain.	Evaluate, compare, and contrast

◖ Analytical Paragraph

___OVERVIEW___ Regardless of whether you go on to study literature, you *will*, if you enter any kind of profession, have to read and write analytically. This page takes you through a sequence of steps that prepare you to write a paragraph in which you analyze some aspect of the text you read.

1. *Establish a focus/purpose to your reading:* Read the assigned pages. Unless told to read for a specific aspect, choose one or two elements from the following list that are most important to the meaning in the passage.

Imagery	Diction	Theme	Tone
Character/Characterization	Setting	Grammar/Syntax	Figurative Language
Rhetorical Strategies	Plot/Structure	Symbols/Allusions	Irony

2. *Read with a purpose in mind and take notes:* As you read, jot down examples, details, observations, and assertions about the meaning, purpose, and effect of the author's choices. Take these notes with the idea in mind that you will use them later as the basis for your analytical paragraph.

3. *Use your notes to write an analytical paragraph:* Your notes should have prepared you to establish a focus (Focus = Subject + Statement about that subject) that you can use and develop into an analytical paragraph. This paragraph should *not* be an informal or personal response but a carefully crafted piece of academic writing worthy of being scored on the SAT or Advanced Placement exams. Your paragraph should have the following:

   Focus: Applies to the paper and to paragraphs and sentences. It combines the *subject* and your *main point* about the subject. It is the controlling idea. In the paragraph you would call it your topic sentence; in the paper you would refer to it as your claim or thesis statement.

   Organization: Refers to how you arrange information throughout the paper and within paragraphs or sentences to achieve a specific effect (e.g., to emphasize). Includes effective transitions from one idea or sentence to the next.

   Development: Refers to two elements: details and commentary. *Details* include the examples, evidence, and quotations you use to support or illustrate your focus. *Commentary* includes analysis, interpretations, insights, opinions, and responses to the question "So what?"

   Purpose: Establishes your intended effect in the paper as a whole and within each paragraph. Writers are always trying to affect a reader's understanding of, attitude toward, or beliefs about a given subject.

© 2007 by Jim Burke from *50 Essential Lessons* (Portsmouth, NH: Heinemann). This page may be reproduced for classroom use only.

Analytical Paragraph Samples

Student Sample: Poetry

"Dream Deferred," by Langston Hughes

Hughes' figurative language adds imagery and emotion to the verse. Five similes follow the question posed at the beginning of the poem, as if someone is suggesting answers. The similes all create unpleasant images in the reader's head. The similes all create unpleasant a festering sore, "rotten meat," (5), and a "heavy load," (10) rather than carefree, light images, like a balloon escaping into the atmosphere. In this way, the reader knows that Hughes views a dream deferred as a grave matter. The poem ends with a metaphor, phrased as a rhetorical question. Because it does not use "like" or "as" to compare the dream to something else, it seems to be meant more literally than the similes. On the page, the line, "Or does it explode?" is its own stanza and is italicized, which emphasizes that idea. The reader can gather from the imagery of the poem that Hughes believes passionately about his dreams and does not easily let them go.

Student Sample: Fiction

Crime and Punishment by Fyodor Dostoevski

Dostoevski uses *Crime and Punishment* to test Raskolnikov's theory of the "extraordinary man" against himself, ultimately showing Raskolnikov (and perhaps anyone) unworthy of any superior status. Considering that Raskolnikov is attractive, intelligent, and a talented writer, it is natural for him to assume that he is one of the select few that he has defined as above the law. However, his criterion for being extraordinary is the merit of one's ideas, of which Raskolnikov has written few. In fact, the only morsel of his philosophy discussed in the novel is the theory itself, thus rendering the argument circular and thus moot. Moreover, Raskolnikov's actions show that he is mentally unable to cope with extraordinary status. First, he mulls over the crime incessantly, unsure of himself. This behavior is not conducive to his belief that he has "the right to transgress the law in any way" (241). He does not even decide to do it until he hears someone echo his sentiment by chance. This weak behavior shows a lack of conviction and an unwillingness to put his money where his mouth is, so to speak. When he does actually manage to vest his actions in his ideas, his illness (as described in his article as the result of a crime) begins almost immediately. Thus, by his own definition, Raskolnikov is not subject to any special treatment.

(I guess the irony in this is that *Crime and Punishment* is a canonized novel and Raskolnikov's struggle for historical greatness has arguably been achieved.)

◆ Analytical Reading

Name: _____

© 2007 by Jim Burke from *50 Essential Lessons* (Portsmouth, NH: Heinemann). This page may be reproduced for classroom use only.

Subject	Meaning	Purpose	Effect
What does the author do?	**What does it mean?**	**Why does the author do this?**	**How does it contribute to meaning?**
• Uses pronouns (without antecedent) throughout beginning of novel to refer to crime he has not committed	• Character cannot even name his planned crime to himself; knows it is wrong and so acts as if he would not do "it"	• Reinforces the forbidden, taboo aspect of his action; wants to show the divided nature of Raskolnikov	• Combined with other elements (e.g., italics and ellipses), the use of such pronouns emphasizes Raskolnikov's attitude toward himself and his crime

Name: _____

◆ Analyzing Symbolism

◆ When reading for symbolic meaning, consider:

- **Context:** What happens before and after?
- **Language:** Does the author use words, sentences, or conventions differently?
- **Imagery:** What colors, objects, or images appear?
- **Tone:** What is the author's (or character's) attitude?

Literal *What it is*	Raskolnikov dreams he is a child walking through graveyard past church he loved with his father.	
Symbolic *What it represents*	Church represents the Christian faith he had in childhood, his pious self; graveyard suggests the death of his faith as an adult. Father symbolizes the protection he had as a child but no longer enjoys as an adult.	
Evidence *Why you think x = y*	Text says he "loved that church," and "reverently crosses himself" at his brother's grave (51). "You are not a Christian!" (53) His father tried to draw him away and said don't look, thus trying to protect him.	
Meaning *Why it's important*	Scene signifies the contrast between the boy he was and the man he has become. The way back to innocence is lost. This provides important back-ground for, and contrast to, what happens later when he takes Lizaveta's cross and bows down at the crossroads, thus trying to regain the humility and innocence he had as a child but denies him-self as an adult.	

◆ When finished, use your notes above to prepare yourself to write a paragraph in which you make a claim about one of the following:

1. *The Author's Craft:* Discuss the author's use of symbols in the text as devices (i.e., how and why does he use them?) OR
2. *The Meaning of the Symbol:* Make an interpretive claim about the meaning of a particular symbol in the text.

Tools and Texts 9

Argument Organizer

Name: _____ Period: _____ Date: _____

Claim
What is the main point you will argue?

⬙ **Claim**

Reason
Why should readers accept your claim?

⬙ **Reason**

Evidence
• Facts
• Figures
• Statistics
• Observations

⬙ **Evidence**

⬙ **Evidence**

⬙ **Evidence**

Acknowledge and Respond
to other perspectives on the subject.

⬙ **Acknowledge**

⬙ **Respond**

Name: _____ Period: _____ Date: _____

◖ **Article Notes**

Title: _____

Author: _____

Subject: _____

◖ **Vocabulary**

1.

2.

3.

4.

5.

Write the definitions on the back.

1. Purpose Question (PQ): Identify the goal.

_____

_____

2. Preview: Gather useful information.

1. _____

2. _____

3. _____

3. Pause and Reflect: List important details and ideas related to your PQ.

1. _____

2. _____

3. _____

4. _____

5. _____

4. PQ: Answer the PQ. What is the subject and the author's main idea about it?

_____

_____

_____

_____

_____

5. Practice Questions: Create two test questions about the subject, article, or author.

1. Factual: _____

2. Inferential: _____

6. Bonus: Post a comment on the board for class discussion.

_____

_____

Name: _____ Period: _____ Date: _____

◖ Book Notes: Essential Information (page 1)

Title

Author

Protagonist and Details
- Conflicts
- Characterizatiion
- Most important character detail
- Author's attitude toward protagonist

(What's most important, and why?)

Antagonist and Details
- Form/Type
- Characterization
- Most important character detail
- Author's attitude toward antagonist

(What's most important, and why?)

Secondary Characters
- Purpose
- Most important minor characters
- Character details
- How main character's actions affect secondary characters

(What's most important, and why?)

Key Plot Details
- Exposition (background)
- Rising action
- Falling action
- Resolution

(What's most important, and why?)

Name: _____ Period: _____ Date: _____

◖ Book Notes: Essential Information (page 2)

Central Themes
- Main Idea
- Topic versus the statement about the truth
- Connection between themes and plot, setting, mood, and tone

(What's most important, and why?)

Setting
- Place
- Time
- Connection to plot, mood, and themes

(What's most important, and why?)

Tone
- Author's attitude toward the subject, characters, or reader
- Description: ironic, sympathetic, gloomy, mysterious

(What's most important, and why?)

Point of View (POV)
- First
- Third
- Omniscient
- Limited
- Purpose/Effect of this POV: i.e., why did the author choose it?

(What's most important, and why?)

Elements of Style
- Language
- Organization
- Diction
- Sentence structure and length
- Devices: imagery, repetition, symbolism, dialogue

(What's most important, and why?)

Bookmark: Reading: Think A

Reading: Think About It!

When reading, remember to:

- Ask questions of the text, yourself, and the author
- Make connections to yourself, other texts, the world
- Use different strategies to achieve and maintain focus while reading
- Determine ahead of time why you are reading this text and how it should be read
- Adjust your strategies as you read to help you understand and enjoy what you read

Evaluating how well you read

Evaluate and decide which of the following best describes your reading performance today.
Explain *why* you gave yourself the score, also.
My reading was:

1. Excellent because I
   - read the full 20 minutes
   - read actively (e.g., used different strategies and techniques)
   - understood what I read
2. Successful because I
   - read almost the entire 20 minutes
   - tried to use some strategies that mostly helped me read better
   - understood most of what I read
3. Inconsistent because I
   - read only about half the time
   - used some strategies, but they didn't help me much
   - understood some of what I read
4. Unsuccessful because I
   - read little or nothing
   - did not read actively
   - did not understand what I read
   - I didn't understand because

Develop your own questions

Develop your own question(s) or prompt(s) that you find helpful when thinking about how or what you read:

Reading: Think About It!

When reading, remember to:

- Ask questions of the text, yourself, and the author
- Make connections to yourself, other texts, the world
- Use different strategies to achieve and maintain focus while reading
- Determine ahead of time why you are reading this text and how it should be read
- Adjust your strategies as you read to help you understand and enjoy what you read

Evaluating how well read

Evaluate and decide which of the following best describes your reading performance today.
Explain *why* you gave yourself the score, also.
My reading was:

1. Excellent because I
   - read the full 20 minutes
   - read actively (e.g., used different strategies and techniques)
   - understood what I read
2. Successful because I
   - read almost the entire 20 minutes
   - tried to use some strategies that mostly helped me read better
   - understood most of what I read
3. Inconsistent because I
   - read only about half the time
   - used some strategies, but they didn't help me much
   - understood some of what I read
4. Unsuccessful because I
   - read little or nothing
   - did not read actively
   - did not understand what I read
   - I didn't understand because

Develop your own questions

Develop your own question(s) or prompt(s) that you find helpful when thinking about how or what you read:

Reading: Think About It!

When reading, remember to:

- Ask questions of the text, yourself, and the author
- Make connections to yourself, other texts, the world
- Use different strategies to achieve and maintain focus while reading
- Determine ahead of time why you are reading this text and how it should be read
- Adjust your strategies as you read to help you understand and enjoy what you read

Evaluating how well you read

Evaluate and decide which of the following best describes your reading performance today.
Explain *why* you gave yourself the score, also.
My reading was:

1. Excellent because I
   - read the full 20 minutes
   - read actively (e.g., used different strategies and techniques)
   - understood what I read
2. Successful because I
   - read almost the entire 20 minutes
   - tried to use some strategies that mostly helped me read better
   - understood most of what I read
3. Inconsistent because I
   - read only about half the time
   - used some strategies, but they didn't help me much
   - understood some of what I read
4. Unsuccessful because I
   - read little or nothing
   - did not read actively
   - did not understand what I read
   - I didn't understand because

Develop your own questions

Develop your own question(s) or prompt(s) that you find helpful when thinking about how or what you read:

Bookmark: Reading: Think B

© 2007 by Jim Burke from *50 Essential Lessons* (Portsmouth, NH: Heinemann). This page may be reproduced for classroom use only.

Reading: Think about It!

Thinking about *how* you read

- I was distracted by…
- I started to think about…
- I got stuck when…
- I was confused/focused today because…
- One strategy I used to help me read this better was…
- When I got distracted, I tried to refocus myself by…
- These words or phrases were new/interesting to me… I think they mean…
- When reading, I should…
- When I read today, I realized that…
- I had a hard time understanding…
- I'll read better next time if I…

Thinking about *what* you read

- Why does the character/author…
- Why doesn't the character/author…
- What surprised me most was…
- I predict that…
- This author's writing style is…
- I noted that the author uses…
- The main character wants/is…
- If I could, I'd ask the author/character…
- The most interesting event/idea in this book is…
- I realized…
- The main conflict/idea in this book is…
- I wonder why…
- One theme that keeps coming up is…
- I found the following quote interesting… _____ this book because…

Elaborating on what you think

- I think _____ because…
- A good example of _____ is …
- This reminded me of because…
- This was important because…
- One thing that surprised me was _____ because I always thought…
- The author is saying that…

Reading: Think about It!

Thinking about *how* you read

- I was distracted by…
- I started to think about…
- I got stuck when…
- I was confused/focused today because…
- One strategy I used to help me read this better was…
- When I got distracted, I tried to refocus myself by…
- These words or phrases were new/interesting to me… I think they mean…
- When reading, I should…
- When I read today, I realized that…
- I had a hard time understanding…
- I'll read better next time if I…

Thinking about *what* you read

- Why does the character/author…
- Why doesn't the character/author…
- What surprised me most was…
- I predict that…
- This author's writing style is…
- I noted that the author uses…
- The main character wants/is…
- If I could, I'd ask the author/character…
- The most interesting event/idea in this book is…
- I realized…
- The main conflict/idea in this book is…
- I wonder why…
- One theme that keeps coming up is…
- I found the following quote interesting… _____ this book because…

Elaborating on what you think

- I think _____ because…
- A good example of _____ is …
- This reminded me of because…
- This was important because…
- One thing that surprised me was _____ because I always thought…
- The author is saying that…

Reading: Think about It!

Thinking about *how* you read

- I was distracted by…
- I started to think about…
- I got stuck when…
- I was confused/focused today because…
- One strategy I used to help me read this better was…
- When I got distracted, I tried to refocus myself by…
- These words or phrases were new/interesting to me… I think they mean…
- When reading, I should…
- When I read today, I realized that…
- I had a hard time understanding…
- I'll read better next time if I…

Thinking about *what* you read

- Why does the character/author…
- Why doesn't the character/author…
- What surprised me most was…
- I predict that…
- This author's writing style is…
- I noted that the author uses…
- The main character wants/is…
- If I could, I'd ask the author/character…
- The most interesting event/idea in this book is…
- I realized…
- The main conflict/idea in this book is…
- I wonder why…
- One theme that keeps coming up is…
- I found the following quote interesting… _____ this book because…

Elaborating on what you think

- I think _____ because…
- A good example of _____ is …
- This reminded me of because…
- This was important because…
- One thing that surprised me was _____ because I always thought…
- The author is saying that…

Character Arc

Name: _____ Period: _____ Date: _____

PART ONE: ANALYZE

DIRECTIONS Characters change over the course of a story; at least the important characters do. But *how* do they change—and *why?* We should also ask which, of all the different changes, is most important—and, of course, *why* it is so important. Use this tool (and these questions) to analyze how the character changes over the course of the story. You should also identify key moments (by indicating them on the arc) that caused the changes along the way.

Beginning

Adjectives or Nouns _____

Adjectives or Nouns _____

End

PART TWO: SYNTHESIZE

DIRECTIONS Use your notes and ideas from Part One to help you write a paragraph in which you synthesize the character's changes and the causes and significance of those changes. Be sure your paragraph has a claim, organizes the information effectively, and provides specific examples that illustrate and support your claim.

_____

_____

_____

_____

_____

_____

_____

◆ Character Development

Name: _____ Period: _____ Date: _____

EARLY ON,...

Focus on what the character:
- ☐ Does
- ☐ Feels
- ☐ Thinks

Include also a discussion of:
- ☐ Reasons (for doing, feeling,...)
- ☐ Causes and effects
- ☐ Importance and implications

Include examples and evidence to:
- ☐ Illustrate your ideas
- ☐ Support your claim(s)

EVENTUALLY, HOWEVER,...

Focus on what the character:
- ☐ Does
- ☐ Feels
- ☐ Thinks

Include also a discussion of:
- ☐ Reasons (for doing, feeling,...)
- ☐ Causes and effects
- ☐ Importance and implications

Include examples and evidence to:
- ☐ Illustrate your ideas
- ☐ Support your claim(s)

IN THE END,...

Focus on what the character:
- ☐ Does
- ☐ Feels
- ☐ Thinks

Include also a discussion of:
- ☐ Reasons (for doing, feeling,...)
- ☐ Causes and effects
- ☐ Importance and implications

Include examples and evidence to:
- ☐ Illustrate your ideas
- ☐ Support your claim(s)

Character Study

DIRECTIONS Choose one of the central characters in the assigned chapter or act. Answer the following questions as you read. Use these details to write a well-organized paragraph that begins with a claim about your character in this chapter/act.

Character's Name: _____ **Chapter/Act:** _____

Background Knowledge

What do you already know about this character?

Why is this detail important?

Plot Details and Character Motivation

What are the key actions for your character?

Why does your character do each of these acts?

Character's Perspective on Self and Others

How does your character feel about these events, other characters, and himself or herself?

Why does your character feel this way?

Others' Perspective on Character

What do others think about your character, and how do their perceptions affect their actions?

Why do they have these thoughts about your character or act as they do in response?

Plot Details: What Changes, and How and Why It Matters

What effect does your character have on the plot as a result of his or her actions in this chapter/act?

Why are these changes important, and how will they affect the rest of the story?

Character Development: Does your character change by the end of the chapter/act? How? Why? *Write a well-organized paragraph on the back.*

Name: _____ Period: _____ Date: _____

Comparison Organizer

Subject A: _____ | **Subject B:** _____

DIRECTIONS

Use these "signal words" when writing your paragraph:

CONTRAST	COMPARE
• although	• again
• but	• also
• however	• similarly
• on the other hand	• likewise
• yet	
• even though	EXAMPLES
• still	• for example
• while	• indeed
• despite	• such as
• on the contrary	• after all
• in contrast	• even
• regardless	• in fact
• though	• for instance
• nonetheless	
• instead	

Subject *(what you will focus on):*

Main Idea *(what you say about the subject):*

_____

_____

_____

Paragraph *(continue on the back of this page):*

_____

_____

_____

_____

_____

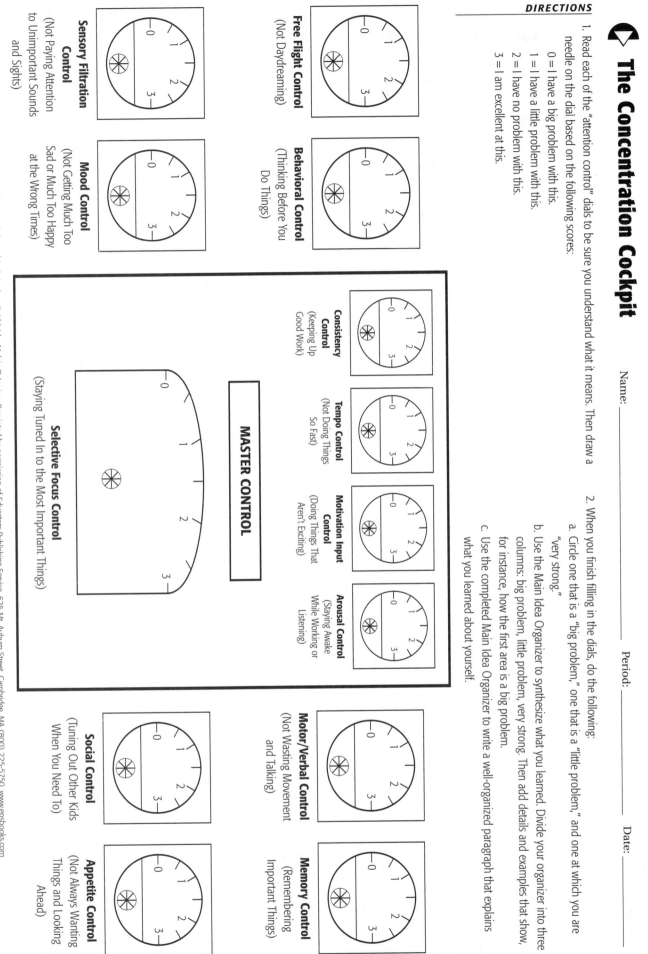

The Concentration Cockpit

© 2007 by Jim Burke from *50 Essential Lessons* (Portsmouth, NH: Heinemann). This page may be reproduced for classroom use only.

Name: _____   Period: _____   Date: _____

DIRECTIONS

1. Read each of the "attention control" dials to be sure you understand what it means. Then draw a needle on the dial based on the following scores:

   0 = I have a big problem with this.
   1 = I have a little problem with this.
   2 = I have no problem with this.
   3 = I am excellent at this.

2. When you finish filling in the dials, do the following:

   a. Circle one that is a "big problem," one that is a "little problem," and one at which you are "very strong."

   b. Use the Main Idea Organizer to synthesize what you learned. Divide your organizer into three columns: big problem, little problem, very strong. Then add details and examples that show, for instance, how the first area is a big problem.

   c. Use the completed Main Idea Organizer to write a well-organized paragraph that explains what you learned about yourself.

Free Flight Control
(Not Daydreaming)

Behavioral Control
(Thinking Before You Do Things)

Sensory Filtration Control
(Not Paying Attention to Unimportant Sounds and Sights)

Mood Control
(Not Getting Much Too Sad or Much Too Happy at the Wrong Times)

Consistency Control
(Keeping Up Good Work)

Tempo Control
(Not Doing Things So Fast)

Motivation Input Control
(Doing Things That Aren't Exciting)

Arousal Control
(Staying Awake While Working or Listening)

MASTER CONTROL

Selective Focus Control
(Staying Tuned In to the Most Important Things)

Social Control
(Tuning Out Other Kids When You Need To)

Motor/Verbal Control
(Not Wasting Movement and Talking)

Memory Control
(Remembering Important Things)

Appetite Control
(Not Always Wanting Things and Looking Ahead)

"Concentration Cockpit" by Mel Levine from *Educational Care*, 2/e by Melvin D. Levine. © 1994 by Melvin D. Levine. Reprinted by permission of Educators Publishing Service, 625 Mt. Auburn Street, Cambridge, MA (800) 225-5750. www.epsbooks.com

◗ Conversational Roundtable

Topic: _____

DIRECTIONS

Ask yourself what the focus of your paper, discussion, or inquiry is. Is it a character, a theme, an idea, a trend, or a place? Then examine it from four different perspectives, or identify four different aspects of the topic. Once you have identified the four areas, find and list any appropriate quotations, examples, evidence, or details.

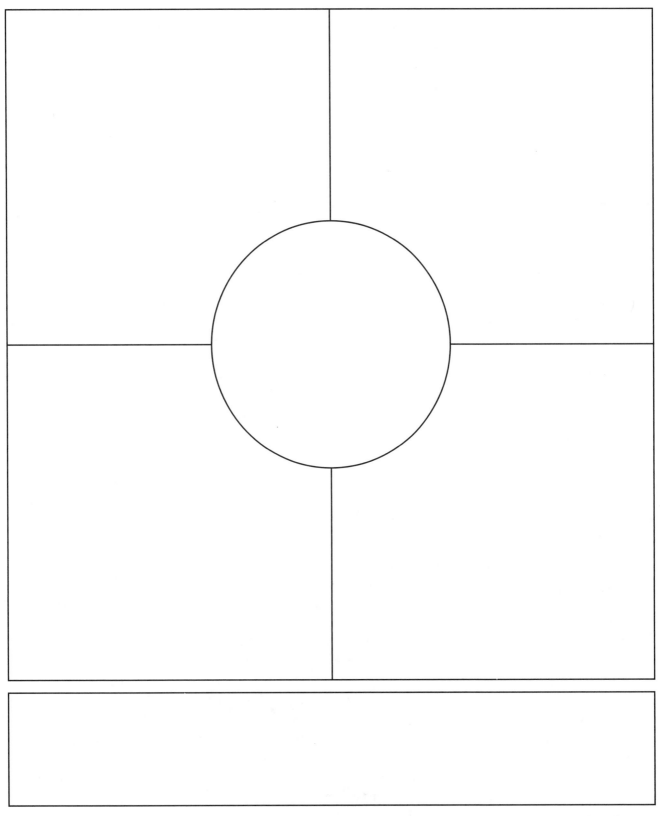

◖ Conversational Roundtable Guidelines

The Four CRT Roles

ASKER

Your role: You *ask* questions about the topic. They should not be yes/no questions, questions whose answer is obvious or a fact. You are the fire-starter. You are extending an invitation to people to *think*. Here are some examples:

- Does _____ have a right to…?
- Is democracy the best form of government?
- Why did _____ behave as it did?

CLARIFIER

Your role: You make comments and ask questions to help the group members better understand their ideas—and the question they are trying to answer. Your responses should extend and support the discussion. Here are some examples:

- Interesting, but is that answering the question…?
- I'm not sure I understand. Can you explain that…?
- Does that mean…?

CONNECTOR

Your role: You connect the current discussion with other topics you've studied or books you've read. Your role is to extend the conversation into new areas that the others might not have considered. Here are some examples:

- When you said…, you reminded me of…
- _____ is a lot like _____ because…
- What is another way to look at that?

VALIDATOR

Your role: Your job is to listen and recognize good ideas or successful participation. Here are some examples:

- That's a really interesting idea, _____ . I hadn't thought of that that way before.
- Oh, that's a good connection. How did you come up with that?
- I like what you said, even though I'm not sure I agree.

Overview

The point with these conversations is not to finish but to *begin*. The group who has the longest, most thoughtful discussion about the fewest questions wins! There are four roles that one person in each group must play (see sidebar).

1. Identify the topic (e.g., "success," "change," "the good life")

2. Formulate a question or statement about it (e.g., "What is success?" "Why do people fear change?" "What is 'the good life'?").

3. Write the question or statement at the top of the page of paper.

4. Generate questions that will help you think about and discuss this topic.

5. Define—in your own words, and using a dictionary—key terms in the statement or question. Be sure to look at the word's etymology (i.e., word history). Here's a sample entry:

   SUCCESS

   SYLLABICATION: suc-cess

   NOUN: **1.** The achievement of something desired, planned or attempted: *attributed their success in business to hard work.* **2a.** The gaining of fame or prosperity: *an artist spoiled by success.* **b.** The extent of such gain. **3.** One that is successful: *The plan was a success.* **4.** *Obsolete* A result or an outcome.

   ETYMOLOGY: Latin *successus*, from past participle of *succdere*, to succeed. See <u>succeed</u>. Middle English *succeden*, from Old French *succeder*, from Latin *succdere*: *sub-*, near; see <u>sub–</u> + *cdere*, to go.

6. Generate contrasting examples that show what the subject (e.g., success) is and *is not*.

7. Use the following questions, along with your own, to support and extend your discussion of the topic:

   - Are there common traits (e.g., of success)?
   - Are there different types (e.g., of success)?
   - Are there different causes (e.g., of success)?
   - Are there different degrees (e.g., of success)?
   - What is the question we are *not* asking—but should?
   - What are three different ways to answer or respond to this question?
   - What assumptions am I making about this topic? (For example, do you assume that "success equals wealth," or that "success is always good"?)
   - What reason do I have for believing something is true or important?
   - What aspects of this topic or question concern, upset, or confuse you?

8. Synthesize your thinking and discussion by doing the following:

   - Choose the question you discussed the most.
   - Sum up your responses to this question.
   - Explain why you thought it was so important or interesting.
   - Explore what you need to keep thinking about this topic or question.

9. Turn in all notes or other evidence of your conversation and work with all group members' names on it.

© 2007 by Jim Burke from *50 Essential Lessons* (Portsmouth, NH: Heinemann). This page may be reproduced for classroom use only.

Name: _____ Period: _____ Date: _____

Cornell Notes (Blank)   Subject: _____ Topic: _____

Name: _____ Period: _____ Date: _____

▷ **Cornell Notes** (Intro)   Subject: _____ Topic: _____

Here, in the **Connections Column,** you might write one or more of the following:

- **Categories**
  - Causes of WWII
  - Parts of a cell
- **Questions**
  - What caused WWII?
  - What are the parts of a cell?
- **Vocabulary words**
  - Holocaust
  - synthesis
- **Review/test alerts!**
  - WWII causes and names of allies will definitely be on exam!
  - Parts of a cell
- **Connections**
  - Check the Owens poem for his comments on war
  - Similar to process we studied in last unit
- **Reminders**
  - Be sure to check the meaning of *variant.*

Sample Question and Notes

What should I write down when I take notes?

> **Note:** Leave space in the *Connections Column* so you can add notes and test review questions later on when studying.

How can I take notes faster?

Write down only important information. Look for:

- bold, underlined, or italicized words
- information in boxes or with an icon/symbol
- headings/subheadings on the page
- information the book or teacher repeats
- words, ideas, or events that might be on a test
- quotes, examples, or details you might be able to use later in a paper or presentation

- abbreviate familiar words/use symbols (+, →, #)
- take notes in bullets and indents, not formal outlines
- cut unnecessary words
- use telegraphic sentences: "America enters war 12/44."

Down here, write one of the following: summary of what you read/lecture; the five most important points of the article/chapter/lecture; questions you still need to answer.

© 2007 by Jim Burke from *50 Essential Lessons* (Portsmouth, NH: Heinemann). This page may be reproduced for classroom use only.

Dense Question Strategy

OVERVIEW

Good readers build meaningful links between what they read and think and the world in which they live. This assignment asks you to generate a basic question that the text can answer, and then add to this some component that links what you are reading to your own experiences, thoughts, beliefs, and opinions. Eventually you create one single question, called a "dense question," about which you can write an essay. In this essay you would write about the intersection between your reading this semester, your life, and the world. Easy stuff! I have provided example questions related to *The Catcher in the Rye*; you should be able to translate these into helpful samples for whatever book you are reading.

Type of Question	Description	Example
TEXT	• information found in text	• Who is the narrator of the story?
READER	• reader's experience, values, ideas	• Have you ever felt fed up with everything and just wanted to take off, get away on your own?
WORLD or OTHER LITERATURE	• knowledge of history, other cultures, other literature	• What other character—in a book or a movie—would you compare the main character to?

SHADED:

TEXT/READER	• combines knowledge of text with reader's own experiences, values, ideas	• What characteristics do you share with the main character?
TEXT/WORLD	• combines knowledge of text with knowledge of history and cultures	• In what ways is Holden similar to teenagers today? In what ways are today's teenagers different?
TEXT/OTHER LITERATURE	• combines knowledge of text with knowledge of other pieces of literature	• How does Holden's relationship with his sister compare with Esperanza's?
READER/WORLD	• combines knowledge of reader's own experiences with knowledge of other cultures, people	• In what ways are teenagers in other countries similar to American teens? In what ways are they different?
READER/OTHER LITERATURE	• combines knowledge of reader's own experiences with other pieces of literature	• In what ways are you similar to and/or different from Holden and Esperanza?

DENSE QUESTION:

TEXT/READER/WORLD or TEXT/READER/OTHER LITERATURE	• combines knowledge of all three areas into one DENSE question	• Why does Holden feel alienated, and how is that related to what many of today's teens feel? Include in your answer a discussion of the extent to which you do or don't share these same feelings, and why.

Text

Reader

World or Other Literature

"Dense Question Strategy" from *Questioning: A Path To Critical Thinking* by Leila Christenbury and Patricia P. Kelly © 1983. Reprinted by permission of the authors.

Name: _____ Period: _____ Date: _____

◗ Direct and Integrated Approaches Exemplars

◗ Direct   The paragraph (or essay) addresses, for example, style head-on:

Dostoevski's style is characterized by its use of several devices that he uses to great effect. Early on he builds the entire narrative around a few key pronouns, none of which have a clear antecedent. In particular, the pronoun *it*, which for the first section of the book refers to his imagined crime,…

The paragraph (or essay) addresses, for example, style within the larger context of some other idea,
◗ Integrated   showing it not in isolation but as an integrated component in a larger pattern of meaning:

Raskolnikov lacks the capacity to imagine himself doing the very act he spends so much time planning. Dostoevski shows this reticence through the character's actions ("he turned slowly and hesitantly toward the bridge") and the very language Raskolnikov uses to refer to his crime. Almost up until the fatal blow, he refers to the act exclusively as "it" or "that"—these pronouns having no evident antecedent that alerts the reader to his intentions. In addition to actions and language, Dostoevski employs what then was a most novel device to provide further insight into Raskolnikov's psyche: his dreams. Soon after the novel begins but before we know what "it" refers to, he crosses the bridge and has a dream in which…

◖ Discussion Cards

◖ Before the Discussion

1. Complete the assigned reading (in or outside of class) and any related assignments.

2. On a 3 x 5 card, generate one discussion question that everyone would be able to respond to—even if they did not complete the assigned reading—but that connects to the text in a meaningful way.

> Example: How is it that one very small group can dominate another group that is ten times larger?
> On some level, does the dominated group have to give control to the controlling group?
> (This question relates to South Africa; *Cry, the Beloved Country;* and *Lord of the Flies.*)

3. Write your response thoughts on the back of the card.

4. Form groups of 4 to 8 participants, keeping your discussion cards in hand.

◖ During the Discussion

5. In the new group, do a read-around of all the questions. Do not read the responses—just the question each person wrote down.

6. Choose two or three questions the group feels are especially useful (i.e., would ensure productive, meaningful discussion).

7. Appoint someone in the group to take notes (keep a record of your group's ideas) during the discussion. Put everyone's name at the top of this paper.

8. Discuss those questions, connecting when possible to the text you have been reading.

9. Choose *one* question from your two or three questions to offer to the full class for follow-up discussion. This should be your group's best question, the one that will yield the best thinking and discussion from the full class.

10. As a class, read aloud the final questions from each group.

11. Engage in a full class discussion, beginning with one of those questions.

12. Connect the discussion to the text.

13. Ask if there are other ways to interpret a passage or see an event.

◖ After the Discussion

14. Using your notes and new ideas from the class discussion, write a well-organized paragraph in which you summarize and respond to the text and the discussion.

15. Turn in all notes and evidence of your work.

Name: _____ Period: _____ Date: _____

▷ Drawing Conclusions Organizer

DIRECTIONS While reading (or after you finish), evaluate the information for importance. Jot down the *three most important pieces of information* (character details, events, etc.) in the Information boxes. In the Conclusion box, write down what conclusion you can draw based on these pieces of information. In the Response box, respond to the conclusion and explain why it is important.

SUBJECT/TITLE: _____

▷ 1. Information _____ **▷ 2. Conclusion**

1.

2.

3.

▷ 3. Response _____

SUBJECT/TITLE: _____

▷ 1. Information _____ **▷ 2. Conclusion**

1.

2.

3.

▷ 3. Response _____

▶ Elements of an Effective Speech or Presentation

◖ Overview

The following ideas are designed to help you speak to either one person (e.g., a coach, a teacher, a prospective employer in an interview) or a large group in a formal setting. Speaking in front of people is considered, by many Americans, the most stressful experience imaginable. These strategies can help ease some of that stress by getting you prepared.

◖ Preparation

First, clarify your topic. Try the business card test: you have only the side of a business card to state your main idea. Aside from that, the following points are essential, even if they do seem obvious.

- Preparation: know your material "cold" so you can worry not about what to say but about how to say it.
- Rehearsal: this might mean walking around your bedroom all afternoon repeating your lines over and over; it might also mean practicing in front of friends, parents, mirrors, even video cameras or tape recorders.
- Audience: how you speak, what you include, and how you act will be determined by the answers to a few simple questions: To whom am I speaking? Why am I speaking to them? What do they know—and what must I explain? How much time do I have?
- Tools and Aids: what, if any, visual or other aids (props, handouts, transparencies, poster, computer presentation, video) should I use to convey this information to my audience most effectively?

◖ Visual Aids

When your purpose is to convey complex or abundant information to your audience, use visual aids to help them keep track of your main ideas. These aids also let the audience know what to expect. For instance, in the example provided below the audience can relax, knowing the speaker will take questions after the presentation.
Consider using one of the following:

- Poster board
- Overhead transparencies (made with colored pens or xeroxed)
- Presentation software such as PowerPoint or Keynote
- Handout with the same information as displayed on your visual aids so listeners don't have to take notes but can pay closer attention or supplement your notes with their own

◖ Characteristics of Effective Speeches or Presentations

- **Visual aids:**
  - Are clearly visible and readable to all members of the audience.
  - Use large basic fonts such as Helvetica for clarity and neatness.
  - Include minimal text for emphasis and readability.
  - Use concrete, precise words that will not confuse the audience.
  - Do not include graphics or images that compete with the information.

- **Effective, engaging speakers:**
  - Pace their speech so that each word gets the proper enunciation and emphasis.
  - Look at their audience as much as possible.
  - Project and inflect their voice in order to engage the audience and emphasize those ideas they feel are particularly important.
  - Use humor or other such devices to engage and maintain their audience's attention.

- **Effective presentations:**
  - Provide an overview of the presentation at the beginning.
  - Provide a summary of the important points in the presentation at the end.
  - Provide strong supporting data or examples to clarify the ideas for the audience.
  - Follow a logical, coherent progression from idea to idea.
  - Avoid any theatrics or other acts that will undermine the speaker's ability to effectively convey the information to the audience.
  - Anticipate the audience's questions and answer them.
  - Restate questions from the audience to clarify (and provide time to compose a thoughtful response to the question).
  - Use transitions to clearly mark where one idea ends and the next begins; these transitions also make for a more fluid, coherent speech.

- **Presentation Strategies:**
  - **Note cards:** these can contain either cue words or main ideas across the top of the card, followed by ideas or scripts as needed.
  - **Outline:** helpful, abbreviated script that supports but allows you to speak instead of read. Also helpful as checklist of what you've discussed.
  - **Memorize:** if you have time, memorize what you will say, especially if you are presenting your information dramatically. Actors reading off 3x5 cards doesn't work too well.
  - **Write your outline or script in larger type and triple-space it** so you don't have to search through the document to find your place.
  - **Have style:** whether this is the handouts, your way of speaking, your humor, or the guiding metaphors and analogies you use to help listeners understand, make sure your speech engages their attention and their heart if at all possible. Give them something to remember.
  - **Avoid words you can easily trip over** during the course of your speech. This is particularly important for speeches that cause stress.
  - **Monitor your audience:** if you see that you are losing them, adjust your speech, improvise, project yourself more forcefully.
  - **Cue words:** on note cards or outlines, such words, if the speaker is well-prepared, allow the speaker to recall all he or she wants to say about a topic. Example: *Implications* signals the memory to recall the list of five different implications for the expanded use of technology in every aspect of our lives.

> - Overview of presentation
> - Background
> - Current status
> - Proposed changes
> - Implications
> - Summary and questions

Name: _____   Period: _____ Date: _____

◖ Episodic Notes

Topic: _____

Purpose: Identify the most important moments; show cause-effect and organization (sequence).

1. Determine the three most crucial stages, scenes, or moments in the story or process.

2. Draw in the box what happens and what you "see" in the text. Be as specific as possible.

3. Remember, these are notes, not works of art: try to capture the action and important details of the moment.

4. Explain (in the Caption section) what is happening and why it is important.

Caption

_____

_____

_____

_____

_____

_____

Caption

_____

_____

_____

_____

_____

_____

Caption

_____

_____

_____

_____

_____

_____

Name: _____ Period: _____ Date: _____

◖ Finals Preparation Checklist (page 1)

Class	Grade	Final Exam Info: Details	Self-Assessment: How Prepared Am I?
1.	**Progress Report 1** **Progress Report 2** **Current** **Goal**		❏ Have *all* quizzes ❏ Have *all* tests ❏ Have (created) review sheet ❏ Have *complete* notes ❏ Know what will be on the final ❏ Know how many questions are on the final ❏ Know what types of questions are on the final ❏ Created study aids: ❏ Study cards ❏ Review sheet ❏ Practice exam ❏ Have a study plan: ❏ Study group ❏ Schedule time with tutor ❏ Have parents/friends quiz me ❏ Meet with teacher for review/help
2.	**Progress Report 1** **Progress Report 2** **Current** **Goal**		❏ Have *all* quizzes ❏ Have *all* tests ❏ Have (created) review sheet ❏ Have *complete* notes ❏ Know what will be on the final ❏ Know how many questions are on the final ❏ Know what types of questions are on the final ❏ Created study aids: ❏ Study cards ❏ Review sheet ❏ Practice exam ❏ Have a study plan: ❏ Study group ❏ Schedule time with tutor ❏ Have parents/friends quiz me ❏ Meet with teacher for review/help
3.	**Progress Report 1** **Progress Report 2** **Current** **Goal**		❏ Have *all* quizzes ❏ Have *all* tests ❏ Have (created) review sheet ❏ Have *complete* notes ❏ Know what will be on the final ❏ Know how many questions are on the final ❏ Know what types of questions are on the final ❏ Created study aids: ❏ Study cards ❏ Review sheet ❏ Practice exam ❏ Have a study plan: ❏ Study group ❏ Schedule time with tutor ❏ Have parents/friends quiz me ❏ Meet with teacher for review/help
4.	**Progress Report 1** **Progress Report 2** **Current** **Goal**		❏ Have *all* quizzes ❏ Have *all* tests ❏ Have (created) review sheet ❏ Have *complete* notes ❏ Know what will be on the final ❏ Know how many questions are on the final ❏ Know what types of questions are on the final ❏ Created study aids: ❏ Study cards ❏ Review sheet ❏ Practice exam ❏ Have a study plan: ❏ Study group ❏ Schedule time with tutor ❏ Have parents/friends quiz me ❏ Meet with teacher for review/help

◖ **Finals Preparation Checklist** (page 2)

Class	Grade	Final Exam Info: Details	Self-Assessment: How Prepared Am I?

5.	**Progress Report 1**
	
	Progress Report 2
	
	Current
	
	Goal
			❏ Have *all* quizzes
			❏ Have *all* tests
			❏ Have (created) review sheet
			❏ Have *complete* notes
			❏ Know what will be on the final
			❏ Know how many questions are on the final
			❏ Know what types of questions are on the final
			❏ Created study aids:
			   ❏ Study cards ❏ Review sheet ❏ Practice exam
			❏ Have a study plan:
			   ❏ Study group
			   ❏ Schedule time with tutor
			   ❏ Have parents/friends quiz me
			   ❏ Meet with teacher for review/help

6.	**Progress Report 1**
	
	Progress Report 2
	
	Current
	
	Goal
			❏ Have *all* quizzes
			❏ Have *all* tests
			❏ Have (created) review sheet
			❏ Have *complete* notes
			❏ Know what will be on the final
			❏ Know how many questions are on the final
			❏ Know what types of questions are on the final
			❏ Created study aids:
			   ❏ Study cards ❏ Review sheet ❏ Practice exam
			❏ Have a study plan:
			   ❏ Study group
			   ❏ Schedule time with tutor
			   ❏ Have parents/friends quiz me
			   ❏ Meet with teacher for review/help

7.	**Progress Report 1**
	
	Progress Report 2
	
	Current
	
	Goal
			❏ Have *all* quizzes
			❏ Have *all* tests
			❏ Have (created) review sheet
			❏ Have *complete* notes
			❏ Know what will be on the final
			❏ Know how many questions are on the final
			❏ Know what types of questions are on the final
			❏ Created study aids:
			   ❏ Study cards ❏ Review sheet ❏ Practice exam
			❏ Have a study plan:
			   ❏ Study group
			   ❏ Schedule time with tutor
			   ❏ Have parents/friends quiz me
			   ❏ Meet with teacher for review/help

Things to Do

What	When	How

Name: _____ Period: _____ Date: _____

Four Core Questions

Association: What goes with what?

Opposition: What opposes/resists what?

Progression: What follows what?

Transformation: What changes into what?

DIRECTIONS Choose one of the four questions above or one *item* within a box to examine in a paragraph.
Begin your paragraph on the lines that follow, continuing onto the back. Be sure to include examples and
quotations to support and illustrate your main idea. Discuss the reason, the process, and the importance.

◖ Icebreaker Speech

◖ BASICS

- 2–3 minutes
- Introduce yourself
- Can read but must be prepared
- Timeline:
  - Outline by end of period
  - Rough draft by end of tomorrow
  - Final draft by _____
  - Rehearse and prepare until speech day
  - Deliver speech and turn in notes

◖ THE ICEBREAKER FOLLOWS THIS OUTLINE:

Introduction
- Who you are
- What you are going to talk about
- Why you are going to talk about this

Body
- Topic 1: e.g., Family (your past/background)
- Topic 2: e.g., Interests (what you like to do)
- Topic 3: e.g., High school and your future career

Conclusion
- What you said
- What you want us to remember
- Thank us for our respect and attention

 Inference Quiz

1. What is the equation for making an inference?

2. Which of the following words BEST describes Father Greg Boyle?
   a. Dangerous
   b. Reckless
   c. Religious
   d. Committed
   e. Popular

3. Use the inference equation to explain how you know the answer in #2.

   What I learned: _____

   What I already knew: _____

   What I inferred: _____

4. List *three* words that describe how the gang members feel about Father Greg.

   _____

   _____

   Choose the *best* of the three words and explain why it best describes him.

   _____

   _____

   _____

   _____

   _____

5. List *three* words that describe how Father Greg feels about the people he works with.

   _____

   _____

   Choose the *best* of the three words and explain how you know this answer.

   _____

   _____

   _____

   _____

   _____

Name: _____ Period: _____ Date: _____

▷ Interactive Notes

Topic: _____

DIRECTIONS   Use Interactive Notes to help you read informational or literary texts. Interactive Notes guide you through a reading process to help you develop your ideas and express them in academic language. You may put questions, comments, connections, or favorite lines in any column. Then use the prompts (or create your own) to help you write.

BEFORE **Prepare to Read**	**DURING** **Question and Comment**	**AFTER** **Summarize and Synthesize**
• List: 　✓ title(s) 　✓ headings 　✓ captions 　✓ objectives 　✓ themes 　✓ words to know • Ask questions • Make predictions • Set a purpose • Decide what matters most	• I wonder why.... • What caused... • I think... • This is similar to... • This is important because... • What do they mean by... • What I find confusing is... • What will happen next is... • I can relate to this because... • This reminds me of... • As I read, I keep wanting to ask...	• Three important points/ideas are... • These are important because... • What comes next... • The author wants us to think... • At this point the article/story is about... • I still don't understand... • What interested me most was... • The author's purpose here is to... • A good word to describe (e.g., this story's tone) is...because... • This idea/story is similar to...

Introduction Evaluation

Name: _____ Period: _____ Date: _____

Introduction Evaluation

1 2 3 4 5	Establishes a compelling focus you must prove
1 2 3 4 5	Establishes your credibility to the reader
1 2 3 4 5	Every sentence serves a specific purpose: no fluff!
1 2 3 4 5	Connects the topic to your reader in a meaningful way
1 2 3 4 5	Conveys the importance of the topic
1 2 3 4 5	Implies or creates an organizational structure for the essay
1 2 3 4 5	Provides an effective transition to subsequent paragraphs
1 2 3 4 5	Addresses the writing prompt (or shows that it clearly will do so)

Comments

Name: _____ Period: _____ Date: _____

Introduction Evaluation

1 2 3 4 5	Establishes a compelling focus you must prove
1 2 3 4 5	Establishes your credibility to the reader
1 2 3 4 5	Every sentence serves a specific purpose: no fluff!
1 2 3 4 5	Connects the topic to your reader in a meaningful way
1 2 3 4 5	Conveys the importance of the topic
1 2 3 4 5	Implies or creates an organizational structure for the essay
1 2 3 4 5	Provides an effective transition to subsequent paragraphs
1 2 3 4 5	Addresses the writing prompt (or shows that it clearly will do so)

Comments

Name: _____ Period: _____ Date: _____

Introduction Evaluation

1 2 3 4 5	Establishes a compelling focus you must prove
1 2 3 4 5	Establishes your credibility to the reader
1 2 3 4 5	Every sentence serves a specific purpose: no fluff!
1 2 3 4 5	Connects the topic to your reader in a meaningful way
1 2 3 4 5	Conveys the importance of the topic
1 2 3 4 5	Implies or creates an organizational structure for the essay
1 2 3 4 5	Provides an effective transition to subsequent paragraphs
1 2 3 4 5	Addresses the writing prompt (or shows that it clearly will do so)

Comments

The Language of Literary Analysis

TONE WORDS
accusatory
admiring
afraid
ambivalent
amused
analytical
angry
annoyed
apathetic
apologetic
approving
audacious
bemused
benevolent
bitter
bored
callous
calm
candid
cautious
childish
cold
comic
compassionate
complimentary
conciliatory
condescending
confident
confiding
confused
contemplative
contemptuous
contented
critical
curious
cynical
derisive
detached
didactic
disappointed
disdainful
disgusted
dismayed
disparaging
dramatic
dreamy
earnest
ecstatic
effusive
elated
elegiac
energetic
enthusiastic
exaggerating
facetious
factual
fanciful
fascinated
flippant
forgiving
forthright

frivolous
giddy
gloomy
grudging
happy
harsh
haughty
hollow
hopeless
horrific
humorous
impartial
impulsive
incisive
indignant
indulgent
informal
informative
insisting
instructive
irate
ironic
irreverent
joking
jovial
joyful
judgmental
learned
lyrical
matter-of-fact
melancholy
mocking
mordant
mournful
nostalgic
objective
optimistic
passionate
patronizing
peaceful
pensive
persuasive
pessimistic
pitiful
plaintive
playful
poignant
pretentious
proud
provocative
puzzled
querulous
reflective
regretful
remorseful
resentful
resigned
respectful
restrained
reverent
sad
sarcastic

sardonic
satiric
satisfied
scornful
sentimental
serene
severe
sharp
silly
sincere
solemn
somber
spiteful
straightforward
strident
superficial
suspicious
sweet
sympathetic
taunting
thoughtful
tired
tolerant
troubled
unsympathetic
upset
urgent
vexed
vibrant
wary
whimsical
wistful
witty
wry
zealous

STYLE WORDS
abstract
argumentative
colloquial
complex
concrete
conversational
descriptive
detached
disingenuous
disjointed
effusive
expository
figurative
homespun
informal
instructive
metaphorical
moralistic
objective
pedantic
plain
poetic
precise
reasoned
scholarly

symbolic
terse
trite
understated
wry

MOOD WORDS
bleak
dark
delirious
dismal
eerie
elegiac
haunting
lonely
ominous
peaceful
playful
quizzical
reproachful
satiric
serene
soothing
suspenseful
tense
threatening
uplifting
whimsical

CHARACTER WORDS
absorbed
aggressive
aloof
ambitious
amorous
anxious
apathetic
argumentative
arrogant
bitter
bored
carefree
careless
cautious
churlish
compassionate
conceited
conniving
curious
deceitful
demure
detached
devious
devoted
dishonest
easygoing
envious
exacting
frantic
fretful
gregarious
intelligent

irritable
loquacious
manipulative
mendacious
naive
nervous
noble
outgoing
patient
picky
scrupulous
self-involved
sincere
sloppy
spontaneous
suspicious
talkative
testy
uninvolved
unpredictable
vindictive
welcoming
wise
worried

DICTION WORDS
abstract diction
concrete diction
connotation
denotation
elevated/formal
low/informal
colloquial
conversational
jargon
slang

SYNTAX WORDS
balanced sentence
complex sentence
compound sentence
compound-complex
  sentence
declarative
exclamatory
imperative
interrogative
interruption
inversion
juxtaposition
loose/cumulative
  sentence
parallel structure
periodic sentence
repetition
rhetorical question
simple sentence

Leonardo da Vinci's Notes:
Visual Explanations and Visual Narratives

Leonardo da Vinci used a vocabulary of both images and words to help him make sense of and make visible the ideas in his head. Through such "studies," he learned and shaped the ideas that led to his final paintings.

Even da Vinci used Cornell Notes, as this page from his journal shows.

Visual Explanations

Visual Narrative: Study for *The Last Supper*

◐ Lit Notes (page 1)

Take Phase 1 notes while reading the story through the *first* time. Take Phase 2 and 3 notes as you reread the story to better understand *what* it means and *how* the author creates that meaning.

Phase 1: Reading for Plot

1. Who are the most important characters, and what role do they play?
2. What is the most important event or development in each chapter?
3. When, why, and how does the story or character change in a major way?

Phase 2: Reading for Meaning

1. What type of story is this: a chronicle or a fable?
   - Is the story set in a realistic world like the one you live in?
   - How does the author present reality: physical or psychological details?
   - Why does the author present the world as he/she does?
   - Does the author combine the realistic and the fantastic? If so, how and why?

2. What does the main (or a secondary) character want most?
   - What prevents him/her from obtaining it?
   - How does each go about overcoming these obstacles to obtain it?

3. Who is telling the story?
   - What POV (point of view) is it told from?
     - First (*I*)
     - Second (*you*)
     - Third (limited, objective, omniscient)
   - Why does the author use that point of view?
   - What is the author's attitude toward the main character(s), and how can you tell?

4. Where does the author set the story?
   - How would you describe the setting? Natural or man-made?
   - How does the environment reflect, respond, or otherwise contribute to the story's meaning?
   - Does the setting or atmosphere change, and if so, how and why?

5. How would you characterize the author's style?
   - *Diction:* What words does the author use? What connotations do these words have? Are the words formal or informal? Colloquial or conversational?
   - *Sentences:* Are the sentences long, short, or both? What type of sentences are they: simple, compound, or compound-complex?
   - *Analysis:* Apply these different techniques to analyze the author's style:
     - The longest sentence in a representative paragraph has _____ words.
     - The shortest sentence in a representative paragraph has _____ words.
     - The average number of words in a sentence in a representative paragraph is ___.
     - The number of nouns with 3+ syllables in a representative paragraph is _____.
     - The number of verbs with 3+ syllables in a representative paragraph is _____.
     - Repeat the same process with three dialogue passages. Then explain:
       – How do characters speak?
       – How does their speech reflect their character or contribute to the meaning of the story?
   - *Effect:* How do the author's choices about style contribute to the story's meaning?

6. How does the author use imagery, symbolism, and figurative language in the story?
   - Are there any repeated objects, colors, places, or seasons?
   - Is a certain image used as a metaphor or symbol? If so, how is it used and for what purpose?
   - How does the author's use of imagery or figurative language contribute to the meaning of the story?

7. How does the story begin and end?
   - How does the opening relate to the story in general? Where is the narrator situated as he/she tells the story?
   - How does it end? Why does the author end it that way?
   - Does the ending suggest the story continues and the characters will keep making the same mistakes?
   - How would you characterize the author's philosophy based on the story and its ending?

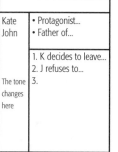

Phase 1 notes

From *The Well-Educated Mind: A Guide To Classical Education At Home* by Jessie Wise and Susan Wise Bauer. © 1999 by Jessie Wise and Susan Wise Bauer. Used by permission of W. W. Norton & Company, Inc.

Lit Notes (page 2)

Phase 3: Reading for Rhetoric

1. Which characters, if any, do you feel sympathy for, and why?

2. How are you similar to or different from the main character(s)?

3. What is the author's perspective on the human condition in this story?

4. What elements contribute most to the character or the story's meaning?

5. What behaviors do the characters engage in, and how do these behaviors provide insight into each character, situation, story, or the world?

6. To what extent does the author respond to, comment on, or otherwise reflect the historical era in which the book is set or in which the author wrote it?

7. What is the author's argument (i.e., the point the author is trying to make about the subject)?

8. How does the character's fate relate to the author's primary argument about the world or the human condition?

9. Do you agree with the author's view of humanity or the world?

10. Is the book true (i.e., accurate) in its portrayal of human nature, society, and the human condition?

11. What does fiction accomplish here that other genres could not? How does it accomplish that?

12. Author Mark Salzman says he writes nonfiction when he wants to "make a documentary" of an experience and writes fiction when he wants to work through a "thought-problem." What is the thought-problem this book explores, and what does the author say about it?

Name: _____ Period: _____ Date: _____

Literature Circle Notes: Overview of the Roles

Discussion Director

Your role demands that you identify the important aspects of your assigned text and develop questions your group will want to discuss. Focus on the major themes or "big ideas" in the text and your reaction to those ideas. What interests you will most likely interest those in your group. You are also responsible for facilitating your group's discussion.

Sample Questions

- What were you thinking about as you read?
- What did the text make you think about?
- What do you think this text/passage was about?
- How might other people (of different backgrounds) think about this text/passage?
- What one question would you ask the writer if you got the chance? Why?
- What are the most important ideas/moments in this text/section?
- What do you think will happen next—and why?
- What was the most important change in this section? How and why did it happen?

Illuminator

You find passages your group would like to/should hear read aloud. These passages should be memorable, interesting, puzzling, funny, or important. Your notes should include not only the quotations but also why you chose them and what you want to say about them. You can either read the passage aloud yourself or ask members of your group to read roles.

Sample Questions

- What is happening in this passage?
- Why did you choose this passage?
- What does this passage mean, or what is it discussing?
- How should you present this passage?
- Who is speaking in this passage?
- What is the most unique aspect of this passage—and why is it unique?
- What did this quotation/passage make you think about when you read it?
- What makes this passage so confusing, important, or interesting?

Illustrator

Your role is to draw what you read. This might mean drawing a scene as a cartoonlike sequence or drawing an important scene so readers can better understand the action. You can draw maps or organizational trees to show how one person, place, or event relates to the others. Explain how your drawing relates to the text. Label your drawings so we know who the characters are. Make your drawing on a separate sheet of paper.

Sample Questions

- What do you think this picture means?
- Why did you choose this scene to illustrate?
- How does this drawing relate to the story?
- Why did you choose to draw it the way you did?
- What do we see—i.e., who and/or what is in this picture?
- What, if anything, did drawing it help you see that you had not noticed before?
- What did this quotation/passage make you think about when you read it?
- What are you trying to accomplish through this drawing?

Connector

Your job is to connect what you are reading with what you are studying or with the world outside of school. You can connect the story to events in your own life, news events, political events, or popular trends. Another important source of connections is books you've already read. The connections should be meaningful to you and those in your group.

Sample Questions

- What connections can you make between the text and your life?
- What other places or people could you compare this story to?
- What other books or stories might you compare to this one?
- What current trends or events are related to this section of the book?
- What other characters or authors might you compare to this one?
- What is the most interesting or important connection that comes to mind?
- What is the connection that no one else but you can discover?
- How does this section relate to those that came before it?

Word Watcher

While reading the assigned section, you watch out for words worth knowing. These words might be interesting, new, important, or used in unusual ways. It is important to indicate the specific location of the words so the group can discuss them in context.

Sample Questions

- Which words are used frequently?
- Which words are used in unusual ways?
- What words seem to have special meaning to the characters or author?
- What new words did you find in this section?
- What part of speech is this word?
- What is the connotative meaning of this word?
- What is the denotative meaning of this word?

Summarizer

Prepare a brief summary of the day's reading. Use the questions to the right to help you decide what to include. In some cases, you might ask yourself what details, characters, or events are so important that they would be included on an exam. If it helps you to organize the information, consider making a numbered list or a time line.

Sample Questions

- What are the most important events in the section you read?
- What makes them so important?
- What effect do these events have on the plot or the other characters?
- What changes—in plot, character, or tone—did you notice when you read?
- What questions about the section you read might appear on an exam?
- What might be a good essay topic for this section of the story?

◖ Literature Circle Notes: Discussion Director

◖ Discussion Director:

Your role demands that you identify the important aspects of your assigned text and develop questions your group will want to discuss. Focus on the major themes or "big ideas" in the text and your reaction to those ideas. What interests you will most likely interest those in your group. You are also responsible for facilitating your group's discussion.

Write your discussion questions (DQs) below. Write your responses to them in the main note-taking area to the right.

Sample Questions

• What were you thinking about as you read?

• What did the text make you think about?

• What do you think this text/passage is about?

• What might other people (of different backgrounds) think about this text/passage?

• What *one* question would you ask the writer if you got the chance? Why?

• What are the most important ideas/moments in this text/section?

• What do you think will happen next—and why?

• What is the most important change in this section? How and why does it happen?

Assignment for today: page _____ to page _____

_____

_____

_____

_____

_____

_____

_____

_____

_____

_____

_____

_____

_____

_____

_____

_____

_____

_____

Topic to be carried over to tomorrow: _____

_____

Assignment for tomorrow: page _____ to page _____

Review, retell, or reflect on what you read so far. (Use the back if necessary.)

Name: _____ Period: _____ Date: _____

◐ Literature Circle Notes: Illuminator

◐ Illuminator:

You find passages your group would like to/should hear read aloud. These passages should be memorable, interesting, puzzling, funny, or important. Your notes should include not only the quotations but also why you chose them and what you want to say about them. You can either read the passage aloud yourself or ask members of your group to read roles.

Write the page and paragraph number in this column. Unless the quote is really long, you should also write the quote in this column. Write your responses to it in the main note-taking area to the right.

Sample Questions

- What is happening in this passage?
- Why did you choose this passage?
- What does this passage mean, or what is it discussing?
- How should you present this passage?
- Who is speaking, or what is happening in this passage?
- What is the most unique aspect of this passage—and why is it unique?
- What did this quotation/passage make you think about when you read it?
- What makes this passage so confusing, important, or interesting?

Assignment for today: page _____ to page _____

_____

_____

_____

_____

_____

_____

_____

_____

_____

_____

_____

_____

_____

_____

_____

_____

_____

_____

Topic to be carried over to tomorrow:

_____

Assignment for tomorrow: page _____ to page _____

Review, retell, or reflect on what you read so far. (Use the back if necessary.)

Name: _____ Period: _____ Date: _____

◖ Literature Circle Notes: Illustrator

◖ Illustrator:

Your role is to draw what you read. This might mean drawing a scene as a cartoonlike sequence or drawing an important scene so readers can better understand the action. You can draw maps or organizational trees to show how one person, place, or event relates to the others. Use the notes area to explain how your drawing relates to the text. Label your drawings so we know who the characters are.

Make your drawing on the back of this page or on a separate sheet of paper, your notes and explanation on the right.

Sample Questions

- What do you think this picture means?
- Why did you choose this scene to illustrate?
- How does this drawing relate to the story?
- Why did you choose to draw it the way you did?
- What do we see–i.e., who and/or what is in this picture?
- What, if anything, did drawing it help you see that you had not noticed before?
- What did this quotation/passage make you think about when you read it?
- What are you trying to accomplish through this drawing?

Assignment for today: page _____ to page _____

_____

_____

_____

_____

_____

_____

_____

_____

_____

_____

_____

_____

_____

_____

_____

_____

_____

_____

Topic to be carried over to tomorrow:

_____

Assignment for tomorrow: page _____ to page _____

Review, retell, or reflect on what you read so far. (Use the back if necessary.)

© 2007 by Jim Burke from *50 Essential Lessons* (Portsmouth, NH: Heinemann). This page may be reproduced for classroom use only.

◖ Literature Circle Notes: Connector

◖ Connector:

Your job is to connect what you are reading with what you are studying in this or other classes. You can also connect the story with events in your own life or the world outside school as depicted in the news or other media. Another valuable source of connections is books you've already read this year. Connections should be meaningful to you and those in your group.

Write your discussion questions below. Write your responses to them in the main note-taking area to the right.

Sample Questions

- What connections can you make between the text and your life?
- What other places or people could you compare this story to?
- What other books or stories might you compare to this one?
- What other characters or authors might you compare to this one?
- What current trends or events are related to this section of the book?
- What is the most interesting or important connection that comes to mind?
- What is the connection that no one else but you can discover?
- How does this section relate to those that came before it?

Assignment for today: page _____ to page _____

_____

_____

_____

_____

_____

_____

_____

_____

_____

_____

_____

_____

_____

_____

_____

_____

_____

Topic to be carried over to tomorrow: _____

_____

Assignment for tomorrow: page _____ to page _____

Review, retell, or reflect on what you read so far. (Use the back if necessary.)

© 2007 by Jim Burke from *50 Essential Lessons* (Portsmouth, NH: Heinemann). This page may be reproduced for classroom use only.

▶ Literature Circle Notes: Word Watcher

▶ Word Watcher:

While reading the assigned section, you watch out for words worth knowing. These words might be interesting, new, important, or used in unusual ways. It is important to indicate the specific location of the words so the group can discuss them in context.

Sample Questions

- Which words are used frequently?
- Which words are used in unusual ways?
- What words seem to have special meaning to the characters or author?
- What new words did you find in this section?
- What part of speech is this word?
- What is the connotative meaning of this word?
- What is the denotative meaning of this word?

In this column, write the word as well as page and paragraph numbers. Write the definition and any explanation about why you chose the word in the notes section to the right.

Assignment for today: page _____ to page _____

_____

_____

_____

_____

_____

_____

_____

_____

_____

_____

_____

_____

_____

_____

_____

_____

_____

_____

Topic to be carried over to tomorrow: _____

_____

Assignment for tomorrow: page _____ to page _____

Review, retell, or reflect on what you read so far. (Use the back if necessary.)

◖ Literature Circle Notes: Summarizer

◖ Summarizer:

Prepare a brief summary of the day's reading. Use the questions to the right to help you decide what to include. In some cases, you might ask yourself what details, characters, or events are so important that they would be included on an exam. If it helps you to organize the information, consider making a numbered list or a time line.

Write your discussion questions below. Write your responses to them in the main note-taking area to the right.

Sample Questions

- What are the most important events in the section you read?
- What makes them so important?
- What effect do these events have on the plot or the other characters?
- What changes—in plot, character, or tone—did you notice when you read?
- What questions about the section you read might appear on an exam?
- What might be a good essay topic for this section of the story?

Assignment for today: page _____ to page _____

_____

_____

_____

_____

_____

_____

_____

_____

_____

_____

_____

_____

_____

_____

_____

_____

_____

_____

_____

Topic to be carried over to tomorrow: _____

_____

Assignment for tomorrow: page _____ to page _____

Review, retell, or reflect on what you read so far. (Use the back if necessary.)

Literature Circle Notes: Illustrator Student Sample

This drawing shows a student's work as Illustrator in a group reading of Mark Mathabane's *Kaffir Boy*.

I drew this picture to show that even though Apartheid still exists, whites and blacks are friends through tennis. Johannes was able to express his opinion openly to whites at a tennis club. The whites there treated him as an equal and accepted the real news of the Soweto riots and the black view of Apartheid.

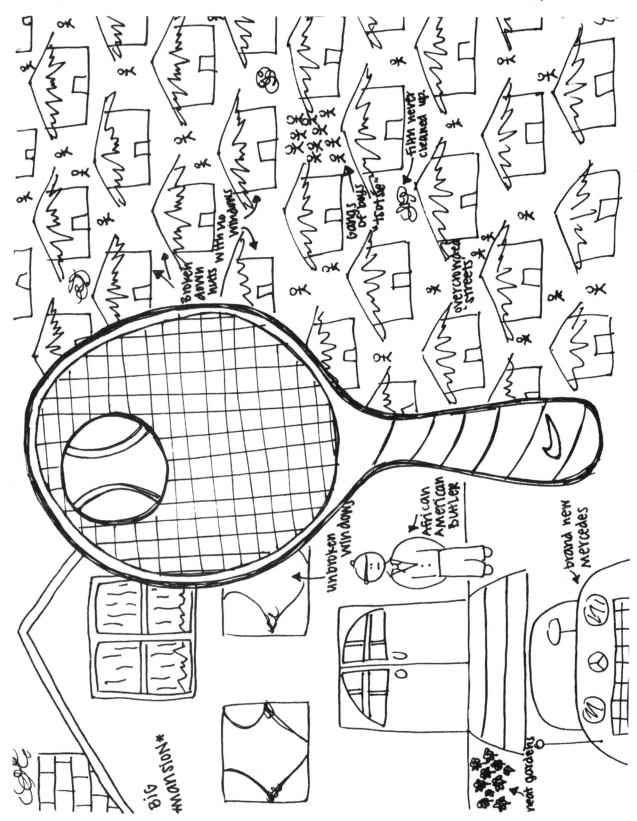

Main Idea Organizer: Reading, Writing, Watching, Listening

Name: _____

© 2007 by Jim Burke from *50 Essential Lessons* (Portsmouth, NH: Heinemann). This page may be reproduced for classroom use only.

Subject
What are you or the author writing about?

Main Idea
What are you (or the author) saying about the subject? (i.e., What is the point you or the author want to make?)

Details
- Examples
- Stories
- Quotations
- Explanations

◐ Subject

◐ Main Idea

◐ Detail

◐ Detail

◐ Detail

◖ Make and Use Study Cards

◖ Overview:

Study cards are like flash cards, but they have more information. They are the perfect tool when you have to learn and *remember:*

- words (e.g., *gamut, au revoir, cytoplast*)
- concepts (e.g., Marxism, meritocracy, abstinence)
- formulas (for converting, determining, calculating)
- events (e.g., signing of the Warsaw Pact, beginning of the Civil War, invention of the cotton gin)

◖ Use the following steps to create and *use* your study cards when preparing for a test:

1. **Assess what you know.** If the teacher gave you a review list, go through it and evaluate what you do and do not know. Put a 1 next to an item if you have no idea what it means; put a 2 next to an item if you have heard of it but can't explain it; put a 3 next to any term that you could explain even if someone woke you up in the middle of the night and asked you.

2. **Make study cards *only* for the 1s and 2s.** Gather as many index cards (with or without lines: your choice!) as you need. Then do the following:

   SIDE *A*:   Words, images, sounds, and sample test questions

   - Put the term on side *A*.
   - Do something visual with it:
     - Use colors for parts of the word
     - Break the word up into pieces (*pro - spects*) (*spect* = to look)
     - Draw symbols or images around the word
   - Write a sample test question for this word or phrase.
   - Write little musical notes near the word to indicate that you have a rhyme, song, or mnemonic to help you remember this term.

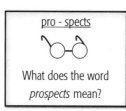

   SIDE *B*:   Definitions, answers, and notes

   - Write the primary definition(s) at the top of side *B*.
   - Write the answer to your sample test question(s).
   - Jot down any notes that will help you remember or better understand the term. *Add to these as you study.*

3. **Manipulate the cards.** The more you do to and with the cards, the better you will understand and remember the information. Remember: Making the cards is not getting ready to study—it is studying. Try these tricks:

   - **Keep adding** notes, symbols, color to them: anything that makes you "process" or think about the idea and makes it stick in your mind.
   - **Shuffle, quiz, and sort:** It's good to change the order of the cards. As you quiz yourself, sort them into "Got it right!" and "Missed it" piles. Now just focus on the ones you keep missing. Periodically, put *all* the cards back into a pile, shuffle them, and quiz yourself. Keep sorting and focusing on the ones you don't remember.
   - **Talk about the material** on the cards. Walk back and forth in your room, explaining each card to yourself. Get together with others and use the cards to focus your discussion.
   - **Play *Jeopardy*** with a study group, a parent, or a sibling. They can pick the cards and quiz you. Example: "What's *inertia* for $500?"
   - **Ask your teacher** how you can remember the difference between, for example, *communism* and *Marxism* if you keep confusing those two.

◖ Making Effective and Efficient Notes

◖ Overview:

Good notes must be complete, coherent, and concise. Whether you are reading, listening, or watching, you must be able to make notes quickly in a format that will be helpful later on when you prepare to write, speak, or take a test.

◖ Page Layout

Divide the page into sections, which serve different purposes. There are four primary spaces you can use to arrange information on the page, as the sample page shows:

◖ Organize Information

Organize information into a visual format that you find helpful. This might include bullets, dashes, or numbers. Though an outline format is helpful, keep it loose so that you don't get confused as you make notes. Identify and organize information into categories that align themselves with chapters, headings/subheadings, major themes, or chronological events; such organization gives your notes structure and coherence. Use additional techniques such as underlining and ALL CAPS to quickly orient your eyes.

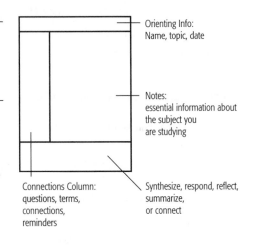

Orienting Info:
Name, topic, date

Notes:
essential information about the subject you are studying

Connections Column:
questions, terms, connections, reminders

Synthesize, respond, reflect, summarize, or connect

BENEFITS OF GOOD NOTES
- **Improve Recall:** Info is better organized, which aids the memory when tested.
- **Increase Understanding:** Organizing info forces you to digest it and establish connections between different ideas.
- **Increase Attention:** Whether reading or listening, taking good notes forces you to pay close attention to what you are studying. It does this by:
    —establishing a purpose   —giving you a focus   —determining what is important

◖ Abbreviate

You are the only one who must be able to use and read your notes. Each class or topic has words and ideas that come up repeatedly. Using symbols, abbreviations, acronyms, or other tricks to condense your notes helps you get down more information in a useful format. Here are some samples and suggestions:

- Shorten familiar words: info for information; NY for New York; WW2 for World War Two
- Use symbols to represent words or ideas: + for *add*; = for *equal*; w/o for *without*; & for *and*; b/c for *because*
- Use acronyms to abbreviate familiar terms: MWH for Modern World History; NATO, GNP, USA, UN, WWI
- Shorten words through omission: gov't for *government*; bldg. for *building*; pps for *pages;* prob for *problem*
- Abbreviate names: A = Atticus; BR = Boo Radley; BE = Bob Ewell; FDR = Franklin Delano Roosevelt
- Shorten common terms: RJ = Romeo and Juliet; Eng = English; OLine = Outline; BStorm = Brainstorm

◖ Telegraph

You do not need to write down *every* word you read or hear. Cut out unnecessary words. Example: "Atticus takes case" or "Germans lose battle; morale worsens."

◖ White Space

Don't crowd your page! Leave space between ideas (e.g., leave an extra space between main ideas). This leaves you room to add information later on and makes your notes easier on the tired eyes trying to read them.

◖ Set Purpose

Decide *why* you are taking notes so you know how to organize your information and evaluate what you should write down. If, for example, you are taking notes for a paper on consequences of a particular historical event, you need to pay special attention to information that might be of possible use. Keep asking yourself: "What is the question these notes are trying to help me answer?" (e.g., What are the primary consequences of...?)

© 2007 by Jim Burke from *50 Essential Lessons* (Portsmouth, NH: Heinemann). This page may be reproduced for classroom use only.

◖ **Making Inferences Organizer**

TITLE: _____

◖ **1. What the Text Says**   ◖ **2. What I Already Know**

_____   _____

_____   _____

_____   _____

◖ **3. What I Infer (about the characters, event, or situation)**

_____

_____

_____

◖ **1. What the Text Says**   ◖ **2. What I Already Know**

_____   _____

_____   _____

_____   _____

◖ **3. What I Infer (about the characters, event, or situation)**

_____

_____

_____

◖ **1. What the Text Says**   ◖ **2. What I Already Know**

_____   _____

_____   _____

_____   _____

◖ **3. What I Infer (about the characters, event, or situation)**

_____

_____

◖ **Respond/Reflect (on the text, the process, your performance)**

_____

_____

_____

_____

© 2007 by Jim Burke from *50 Essential Lessons* (Portsmouth, NH: Heinemann). This page may be reproduced for classroom use only.

Making the Connection

DIRECTIONS

1. Read your assigned text.
2. Before, during, or after you read, jot down connections in the three columns.
3. When you have finished reading, choose one subject. Then write it in the "Subject" box below.
4. Generate three questions about that topic.
5. State your main idea about the subject.
6. Using those questions to guide you, write a well-organized and developed paragraph about that subject with examples or quotations from the text to illustrate your point.

Personal Connections	Text Connections	Other Text or World Connections

Subject _____

_____

Questions about your subject: who, what, where, when, why, how, so what?

1. _____

2. _____

3. _____

Main Idea _____

_____

_____

_____

Paragraph _____

_____

_____

_____

_____

_____

_____

 **Narrative Design**

DIRECTIONS Analyze the narrative design of the story, dividing it into the "primary narrative events" that form the spine of the story and the "secondary elements" that interrupt or otherwise contribute to the story. Only *essential* events and elements should be included.

Chapter/Page	digression • flashback • exposition • interjection / purpose • effect	event • action • development / purpose • effect • meaning	Chapter/Page

Secondary Elements

Primary Narrative Events

AFTER: Analyze the structure for elements of meaningful design. How is it organized? What recurring patterns do you notice? How does one chapter relate to another? How does the beginning relate to the end? What content or constructs run throughout the text? Why?

Name: _____ Period: _____ Date: _____

◖ Organizational Patterns

Organizational Patterns	Symbol	When to Use	Signal Words
1. Sequential Arranged in the order that events occur. Also known as **time order** or **chronological order.**	1. 2. 3.	Narration Exposition Persuasion	*first, begin, while, next, after, following, finally, later, last, then*
2. Spatial Arranged according to location or geographic order. Also known as **geographical order.**	N, L, R, S diagram	Exposition Narration	*inside, outside, next to, behind, beyond, above, near, front, below, left, right, under, east, over, among, between, within*
3. Classification Organized into categories or groups according to various traits.	Boys / Girls boxes	Exposition Persuasion	*type, kind, category, sort, group, trait, feature, characteristic, element*
4. Listing Arranged in a list with no consideration for other qualities.	• ----- • ----- • ----- • -----	Exposition Persuasion	*another, moreover, also, similar*
5. Cause-Effect Arranged to show connections between a result and the events that preceded it. Similar to **problem-solution.**	Cause → Effect, Effect, Effect	Narration Exposition Persuasion	*because, as, since, consequently, caused, inspired, led to, begin, so, therefore, onset, if–then, because*
6. Order of Degree Organized in order of importance, value, or some other quality. Also known as **order of importance.**	triangle	Exposition Persuasion	*most, least, main, primary, lesser, greater, superior, essential, crucial*
7. Comparison-Contrast Organized to emphasize similarities and differences.	Venn diagram	Exposition Persuasion	*however, while, unless, although, like, different, on the other hand, similarly, not only–but also, yet, by contrast, despite, same*
8. Mixed Organized using a blend of patterns. Might, for example, classify groups while also comparing or contrasting them.		Narration Exposition Persuasion	Select as needed from the above lists.

© 2007 by Jim Burke from *50 Essential Lessons* (Portsmouth, NH: Heinemann). This page may be reproduced for classroom use only.

Name: _____ Period: _____ Date: _____

◖ **Paraphrase Prep**

DIRECTIONS

Use this tool to prepare to write a paraphrase of a short text or passage in a longer text. Don't confuse a paraphrase with a summary.

A paraphrase:

- provides a detailed version of the text you paraphrase
- uses the writer's own words to restate what the original text says
- is usually as long as the original text
- is appropriate when the original text is very difficult, often due to technical or antiquated language
- includes all the key points of the original passage
- sounds like *you*, not the original author
- must be cited to indicate its original source
- does not quote or otherwise use the langauge of the original text

Title: _____

Author: _____

Source Info: (Publication, pages) _____

Name: _____ Period: _____ Date: _____

◖ Personal Progress Report (page 1)

DIRECTIONS   Complete the following evaluation of your performance so far this semester. The more honest you are, the more you will benefit from this activity. Please be as specific as possible.

Class:		Teacher:	Grade:
Habits of Success		**What Helped? What Hurt? What Was Hard?**	
1. Completed all assignments?	Y / N		
2. Did my best on *all* work?	Y / N		
3. Turned it all in?	Y / N		
4. Arrived *on time* to class *every* day?	Y / N		
5. Had materials *every* day?	Y / N		
6. Participated in class discussion?	Y / N		
7. Talked to my teacher at least once?	Y / N		
8. Wrote *all* assignments down in planner?	Y / N		
9. Took a risk in class?	Y / N		
10. Came to class *every day* (no absences)?	Y / N		

Class:		Teacher:	Grade:
Habits of Success		**What Helped? What Hurt? What Was Hard?**	
1. Completed all assignments?	Y / N		
2. Did my best on *all* work?	Y / N		
3. Turned it all in?	Y / N		
4. Arrived *on time* to class *every* day?	Y / N		
5. Had materials *every* day?	Y / N		
6. Participated in class discussion?	Y / N		
7. Talked to my teacher at least once?	Y / N		
8. Wrote *all* assignments down in planner?	Y / N		
9. Took a risk in class?	Y / N		
10. Came to class *every day* (no absences)?	Y / N		

Class:		Teacher:	Grade:
Habits of Success		**What Helped? What Hurt? What Was Hard?**	
1. Completed all assignments?	Y / N		
2. Did my best on *all* work?	Y / N		
3. Turned it all in?	Y / N		
4. Arrived *on time* to class *every* day?	Y / N		
5. Had materials *every* day?	Y / N		
6. Participated in class discussion?	Y / N		
7. Talked to my teacher at least once?	Y / N		
8. Wrote *all* assignments down in planner?	Y / N		
9. Took a risk in class?	Y / N		
10. Came to class *every day* (no absences)?	Y / N		

Personal Progress Report (page 2)

Class:		Teacher:	Grade:
Habits of Success		**What Helped? What Hurt? What Was Hard?**	
1. Completed all assignments?	Y / N		
2. Did my best on *all* work?	Y / N		
3. Turned it all in?	Y / N		
4. Arrived *on time* to class *every* day?	Y / N		
5. Had materials *every* day?	Y / N		
6. Participated in class discussion?	Y / N		
7. Talked to my teacher at least once?	Y / N		
8. Wrote *all* assignments down in planner?	Y / N		
9. Took a risk in class?	Y / N		
10. Came to class *every day* (no absences)?	Y / N		

Class:		Teacher:	Grade:
Habits of Success		**What Helped? What Hurt? What Was Hard?**	
1. Completed all assignments?	Y / N		
2. Did my best on *all* work?	Y / N		
3. Turned it all in?	Y / N		
4. Arrived *on time* to class *every* day?	Y / N		
5. Had materials *every* day?	Y / N		
6. Participated in class discussion?	Y / N		
7. Talked to my teacher at least once?	Y / N		
8. Wrote *all* assignments down in planner?	Y / N		
9. Took a risk in class?	Y / N		
10. Came to class *every day* (no absences)?	Y / N		

Class:		Teacher:	Grade:
Habits of Success		**What Helped? What Hurt? What Was Hard?**	
1. Completed all assignments?	Y / N		
2. Did my best on *all* work?	Y / N		
3. Turned it all in?	Y / N		
4. Arrived *on time* to class *every* day?	Y / N		
5. Had materials *every* day?	Y / N		
6. Participated in class discussion?	Y / N		
7. Talked to my teacher at least once?	Y / N		
8. Wrote *all* assignments down in planner?	Y / N		
9. Took a risk in class?	Y / N		
10. Came to class *every day* (no absences)?	Y / N		

Successes	**Disappointments**

Name: _____ Period: _____ Date: _____

Personal Reading Assessment

Week of: _____

Pages		Days of the Week				Total Pages:	Daily Average:	
	M	T	W	Th	Fri	Title(s)	Evaluation	
20							• Completion	
15							• Effort	
10							• Development	
5							• Insight (Reflection)	
0							Score:	(out of 10)

1. Weekly Reflection

- What did you do well as a reader? _____
- What was difficult for you–and why? _____
- Strategies you used? _____

2. Factual Question (AKA "Right There" Question)

Question _____

_____

Importance _____

_____

_____

Answer (include page number) _____

_____

3. Inferential Question (AKA "Author and You" or "Think and Search" Question)

Question _____

_____

Importance _____

_____

_____

Answer (include page number) _____

_____

4. Essay Question (Based on the text you read this week)

Question _____

_____

Importance _____

_____

5. Vocabulary Words (Based on the text you read this week)

Word	Definition (*in your own words* but based on dictionary entry)
1.	
2.	
3.	
4.	
5.	

| 1: | 2: | 3: | 4: | 5: | Total: |

◖ Plot Notes

OVERVIEW

1. **Exposition:** Background information that establishes the setting and describes the situation in which the main characters find themselves.
2. **Rising action:** Characters face or try to solve a problem. This results in conflicts within themselves or with others; these conflicts grow more intense and complicated as the story unfolds.
3. **Climax:** Eventually the story reaches a crucial moment when the characters must act.
4. **Falling action:** Sometimes called the denouement, this part of the story explores the consequences of the climactic decision. The reader feels the tension in the story begin to ease.
5. **Resolution:** The story's central problem is finally solved, leaving the reader with a sense of completion, though the main characters may not feel the same way.

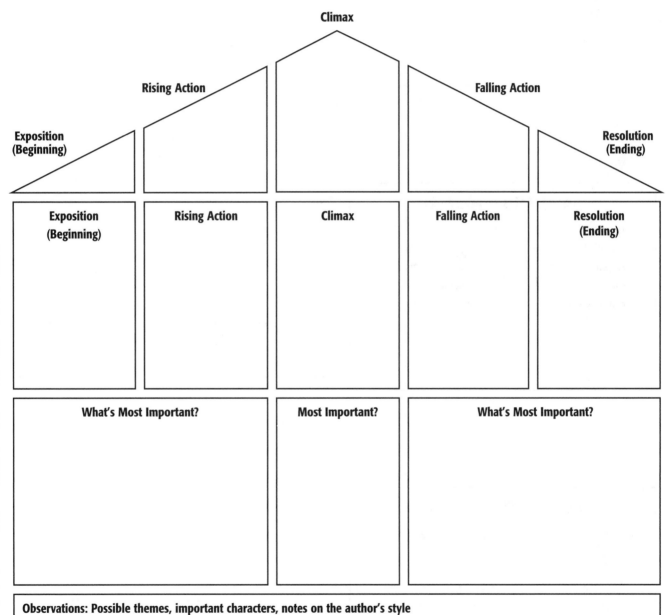

Exposition (Beginning)	Rising Action	Climax	Falling Action	Resolution (Ending)

What's Most Important?	Most Important?	What's Most Important?

Observations: Possible themes, important characters, notes on the author's style

Name: _____ Period: _____ Date: _____

▶ Presentation Slides (page 1)

DIRECTIONS _____ In response to each slide, note points or ideas to use when you create your own presentation.

PRESENTING INFORMATION

Strong presentations are:	Weak presentations are:
– Focused	– Vague
– Engaging	– Boring
– Relevant	– Irrelevant
– Coherent	– Incoherent
– Insightful	– Obvious

Notes:

_____

_____

_____

_____

_____

_____

_____

GAME SHOW FORMAT

• Advantages
- Potentially entertaining
- Helpful structure
- Familiar
- Fun (to create)

• Disadvantages
- Usually distracting
- Lose their focus
- Superficial
- Boring (for audience)

Notes:

_____

_____

_____

_____

_____

_____

_____

VIDEO PRESENTATIONS

• Advantages
- Control of product
- Fun
- Special effects
- Don't have to speak in front of the class

• Disadvantages
- Ineffective
- Boring to watch
- Distracting
- Demand lots of time outside of class

Notes:

_____

_____

_____

_____

_____

_____

_____

Name: _____ Period: _____ Date: _____

◖ Presentation Slides (page 2)

<table>
<tr><td>

POWERPOINT PRESENTATIONS

- **Advantages**
  - Organized
  - Focused
  - Effective
  - Support multiple media

- **Disadvantages**
  - Must be able to speak with few notes
  - Need computer
  - Potentially dull
  - Require skills

</td><td>

Notes:

_____

_____

_____

_____

_____

_____

_____

</td></tr>
</table>

<table>
<tr><td>

TALK SHOW FORMAT

- **Advantages**
  - Structured
  - Appropriate
  - Potentially engaging
  - Informative

- **Disadvantages**
  - Distracting
  - Ineffective
  - Potentially dull
  - Potentially incoherent

</td><td>

Notes:

_____

_____

_____

_____

_____

_____

</td></tr>
</table>

<table>
<tr><td>

CONCLUSION

- **You should**
  - Choose carefully
  - Be comfortable
  - Provide succinct synopsis of contrasts
  - Offer support
    - Use board
    - Provide handout
    - Use overhead

- **You should NOT**
  - Mistake entertainment for information
  - Worry: We want you to succeed
  - Read to us
  - Assume we undertand

</td><td>

Notes:

_____

_____

_____

_____

_____

_____

</td></tr>
</table>

◗ Q Notes

OVERVIEW

Q Notes combine two well-known and powerful methods: SQ3R and Cornell Notes. I call this tool "Q Notes" because you can only write **Q**-uestions in the left-hand margin; when you prepare for a **Q**-uiz, the **Q**-uestions serve as **CUES** to remind you what you must know. When using these notes to study, fold the right edge of the paper over so that it lines up with the dotted line. You should then only be able to see your questions in the **Q**-column. Use these to **Q**-uiz yourself.

Directions:

Turn the titles, subheadings, and topic sentences into questions in this column.

Directions:

In this area, write the answers to the questions. Use bullets and dashes to help organize your ideas. Also, use symbols and abbreviations to help you take notes more efficiently.

Here you should review, retell, or reflect on what you read so far.

Continue on the back.

Name: _____ Period: _____ Date: _____

◖ Reading Process Self-Evaluation

◖ BEFORE

1.	I gather any materials (highlighter, notebook, sticky notes, etc.) I might need.	Always	Usually	Sometimes	Rarely	Never
2.	I choose a place without distractions to do my reading.	Always	Usually	Sometimes	Rarely	Never
3.	I make sure I have a dictionary within reach.	Always	Usually	Sometimes	Rarely	Never
4.	I go over any directions for the assigned reading.	Always	Usually	Sometimes	Rarely	Never
5.	I preview (skim) the assignment to determine what it's about, how long it will take me, and how hard it is.	Always	Usually	Sometimes	Rarely	Never
6.	I make a plan for how to take notes based on the assignment.	Always	Usually	Sometimes	Rarely	Never
7.	I generate a purpose question about the text.	Always	Usually	Sometimes	Rarely	Never
8.	I make predictions about what I will read before beginning.	Always	Usually	Sometimes	Rarely	Never
9.	I ask myself what I already know about this subject, this story, or this author.	Always	Usually	Sometimes	Rarely	Never
10.	I decide which reading strategy/strategies will be most useful.	Always	Usually	Sometimes	Rarely	Never

◖ DURING

11.	I revisit my purpose and make sure I look for the information that will help me achieve it.	Always	Usually	Sometimes	Rarely	Never
12.	I make connections to myself, the world, and other texts/studies.	Always	Usually	Sometimes	Rarely	Never
13.	I identify the main idea and supporting details.	Always	Usually	Sometimes	Rarely	Never
14.	I use previous experience and background knowledge to understand new information about the subject or story.	Always	Usually	Sometimes	Rarely	Never
15.	I take notes, annotate the text, or highlight important details.	Always	Usually	Sometimes	Rarely	Never
16.	I keep a list of questions about things I do not understand.	Always	Usually	Sometimes	Rarely	Never
17.	I look up words I do not understand in the dictionary.	Always	Usually	Sometimes	Rarely	Never
18.	I summarize what I read (in my head and/or in my notes) as I go.	Always	Usually	Sometimes	Rarely	Never
19.	I make predictions about what will happen.	Always	Usually	Sometimes	Rarely	Never
20.	I monitor my understanding as I go and stop to use various "fix-up" strategies when I get confused.	Always	Usually	Sometimes	Rarely	Never
21.	I ask questions about what I read as I go.	Always	Usually	Sometimes	Rarely	Never

◖ AFTER

22.	I stop and ask whether I know the answer to the purpose question I asked when I first began reading.	Always	Usually	Sometimes	Rarely	Never
23.	I reread all or part of the text to answer remaining questions, examine the author's style, or review for tests.	Always	Usually	Sometimes	Rarely	Never
24.	I evaluate all that I read to determine what is most important to remember in the future (e.g., for tests, papers, discussions).	Always	Usually	Sometimes	Rarely	Never
25.	I use one or more strategies to help remember these details.	Always	Usually	Sometimes	Rarely	Never

DIRECTIONS _____ **Reading Improvement Plan**

Based on your evaluation above, make a plan for what you will do to improve your reading performance. In your plan, identify three to five actions that you can take immediately to get rapid results; then discuss how you will accomplish your plan and why it will make a difference.

© 2007 by Jim Burke from *50 Essential Lessons* (Portsmouth, NH: Heinemann). This page may be reproduced for classroom use only.

◐ Reflective Reading Quiz

1. Generate *five* words that best describe _____ in _____ .

These should be words that capture not just what he does but why he does it; what he is like; and how he acts, thinks, and feels.

2. Evaluate those five words and choose the *one* word that best describes _____ in _____.

3. Generate a claim in which you apply that word to_____ , explaining why this is the *best* word and providing examples

from the text to illustrate and support what you say. Be sure to show how this word applies not only to what _____

is like but also to what he does (i.e., key actions or events) in _____.

4. Turn in your paragraph.

---

5. Get into groups, and using the words you generated for the quiz, begin a discussion about _____.

6. Evaluate all the different words people finally chose for their one word on the quiz. Then choose the *one* word your group will offer to the class as

the single best word to describe _____.

7. Enter into a full class discussion guided by these words from step 6.

◐ **Reflective Reading Quiz Exemplar**

1. Generate *five* words that best describe <u>Raskolnikov</u> in <u>Part One</u>. These should be words that capture not just what they do but why they do it; what they are like; and how they act, think, and feel.

2. Evaluate those five words and choose the *one* word that best describes <u>Raskolnikov</u> in <u>Part One</u>.

3. Generate a claim in which you apply that word to <u>Raskolnikov</u>, explaining why this is the *best* word and providing examples from the text to illustrate and support what you say. Be sure to show how this word applies not only to what <u>Raskolnikov</u> is like but also to what they do (i.e., key actions or events) in <u>Part One.</u>

4. Turn in your paragraph.

---

5. Get into groups, and using the words you generated for the quiz, begin a discussion about <u>Raskolnikov</u>.

6. Evaluate all the different words people finally chose for their one word on the quiz. Then choose the *one* word your group will offer to the class as the single best word to describe <u>Raskolnikov</u>.

7. Enter into a full class discussion guided by these words from step 6.

Name: _____   Period: _____   Date: _____

▶ Reporter's Notes

Topic: _____

DIRECTIONS

Reporter's Notes helps you get the crucial information—not "just the facts, Ma'am," but the meaning of the facts, too. These are the questions all reporters ask when they write their articles. These are the questions that good readers ask. Not all questions are always appropriate; you decide whether it's okay to leave one or more blank, but be sure you can explain why that information is absent.

WHO (is involved or affected)	**Most Important WHO**
WHAT (happened)	**Most Important WHAT**
WHERE (did it happen)	**Most Important WHERE**
WHEN (did it happen)	**Most Important WHEN**
HOW (did they do it or did others respond)	**Most Important HOW**
WHY (did they do this, react this way)	**Most Important WHY**
SO WHAT? (Why is this event/info/idea important?)	**Most Important SO WHAT?**

 # Rhetorical Notes

What is the Subject?	

What is the author's claim, or main idea, about this subject?
• Name
• Author
• Genre
• Title
• Date
• Rhetorical Verb
  • *Argues*
  • *Claims*
  • *Suggests*
  • (Or similar verbs)
	(Write it as a statement using the guidelines listed to the left.)

List three key points (quotations or examples) the author makes to illustrate and/or support this claim.	
How does the author develop and support this claim? Focus on: • Strategies • Devices • Organization	
What is the author's purpose? *The author attempts to persuade the reader to…* *in order to…*	

Summarize the author's argument, focusing on the subject, purpose, and rhetorical strategies used to achieve that purpose.

_____

_____

_____

_____

_____

_____

_____

_____

Continue on the back

Name: _____ Period: _____ Date: _____

▶ Speaker Notes

1. What is the speaker's name? _____

2. What organization or business does the speaker represent? _____

3. What is the speaker's area of expertise? _____

4. What is the subject of the speaker's talk? _____

5. List three questions you would like to ask the speaker about this subject.

1. _____

_____

2. _____

_____

3. _____

_____

6. Write down two comments the speaker made that interested you or seemed very important.

1. _____

_____

2. _____

_____

7. List some key words that came up during the speaker's presentation.

8. What was the speaker's *main point* about this subject?

9. On a scale of 1 to 10, how effective was the speaker's presentation? Explain your score.

10. Write a brief response to the speaker and the subject that the speaker discussed. (Write on back.)

Name: _____ Period: _____ Date: _____

▷ Speech Evaluation

▷ CATEGORY	▷ SCORE	▷ COMMENTS
Subject		
Focus (5) • Your speech has *one* subject. • You establish your focus (main idea) clearly and effectively. • Each part of your speech (introduction, body, and conclusion) has a specific focus.		
Organization (5) Your speech: • Uses one or more organizational patterns • Maintains organization throughout the speech • Has an introduction, body, and conclusion		
Development (5) You develop the ideas in your speech by using: • Supporting details • Examples • Stories • Explanations		
Ethos (5) • *Likeableness:* You had a friendly, positive attitude when speaking; you won over the audience. • *Integrity:* You were honest, credible, and conscientious. • *Forcefulness:* You were confident, enthusiastic, and in control of yourself. • *Competence:* You were prepared, and you knew your topic well.		
Completion (5) You satisfied all requirements regarding: • Time • Subject • Type of speech		
TOTAL SCORE (OUT OF 25)		

Name: _____ Period: _____ Date: _____

▷ Speech Prep Notes

	Introduction
▷ SUBJECT	
What are the main ideas you will discuss in your speech?	1.
Consider opening with:	
• an interesting question	2.
• a good/funny story	
• a demonstration	
• a strong statement	3.
• a prop or visual aid	

	Body
▷ FIRST IDEA	
• *Focus* on *one* idea.	
• *Organize* your ideas by:	
• Time Order	
• Geographic Order	
• Importance	
• Cause-Effect	
• Comparison-Contrast	
• Classification Order	
• *Develop* your ideas with:	
• Details	
• Examples	
• Stories	
▷ SECOND IDEA	
• *Focus* on *one* idea.	
• *Organize* your ideas by:	
• Time Order	
• Geographic Order	
• Importance	
• Cause-Effect	
• Comparison-Contrast	
• Classification Order	
• *Develop* your ideas with:	
• Details	
• Examples	
• Stories	
▷ THIRD IDEA	
• *Focus* on *one* idea.	
• *Organize* your ideas by:	
• Time Order	
• Geographic Order	
• Importance	
• Cause-Effect	
• Comparison-Contrast Order	
• Classification Order	
• *Develop* your ideas with:	
• Details	
• Examples	
• Stories	

	Conclusion
• What are the main ideas you want us to remember?	
• Why is this topic important to you, the audience, or society?	
• Try to end with a final story, image, or memorable statement.	

Name: _____ Period: _____ Date: _____

◖ **Structured Response Notes**

_____ **DIRECTIONS**   While reading the assigned text, choose one of the three structured response sequences to help you read and prepare to write about or discuss the text.

I	II	III
What	*Who*	*Who*
changed	• thinks • feels • wants — *what* • says	did *what*
in what *way*	in what *context*	to *whom*
for what *reason*	for what *reason*	in what *context*
to what *effect*	and to what *effect?*	for what *reason*
and why is this change *important?*	*How* do you know this? (What evidence from the text can you provide, and how does it relate?)	and to what *effect?*
How do you know this? (What *evidence* from the text can you provide?)	Why (and to whom) is this *important?*	Finally, *why* is it important?

◖ Use the questions above to synthesize your ideas about a passage, character, or text. Use the space below and continue on the back. Otherwise, use the Structured Response Notes to help you write in your Reader's Notebook.

_____

_____

_____

STUDENT WEEKLY PLANNER

I want to learn more about: _____

Date: _____

Weekly Goal:

Steps to Success:

Opportunities/Appointments/Tests

DAY	TIME	EVENT

INTEGRITY

KNOWLEDGE · SKILLS

CREATIVITY · LEADERSHIP · ATTITUDE

INITIATIVE · DISCIPLINE · PURPOSE · PREPARATION

ELEMENTS OF SUCCESS

DATE DUE	ASSIGNMENT	PRIORITY	DONE

CLASS	GRADE	WHAT I NEED TO IMPROVE AND HOW CAN I DO THAT? WHO CAN HELP?

▶ At the end of the week, **revisit your goal**. Did you achieve it? Use the back of this sheet to write **why** or **why not.**

◖ Style Analysis Notes

◖ Domain	Questions to Ask
Imagery Sensory details Symbols Allusions Words/Phrases Effect/Intent Connection to: 　Mood/Tone 　Theme 　Plot 　Character	• What sensory information do I find in the language: colors, scents, sounds, tastes, or textures? • What is the author trying to convey or achieve by using this imagery? • Are these images part of a larger pattern or structure within the text (e.g., do the images connect to one of the major themes)? • What figures of speech–metaphors, similes, analogies, personification–does the writer use? How do they affect the meaning of the text? What is the author trying to accomplish by using them?
Diction Types 　Slang 　Colloquial 　Jargon 　Dialect 　Formal 　Concrete 　Abstract 　Denotation 　Connotation	• Which of the following categories BEST describes the diction in the passage or text? 　• Informal (e.g., dialect, slang, or jargon) 　• Formal 　• Abstract or concrete 　• Denotative (direct) or connotative (suggestive) • What effect is the author trying to achieve through the use of a specific type of diction? • What does the author's use of diction suggest about his or her attitude toward the subject, event, or character? • What are the connotations of a given word used in a particular context? (To begin, you might ask if particular words have a positive or negative connotation and then consider them in the specific context.) • What words would best describe the diction in a specific passage or the text in general?
Syntax Sentence structure Sentence patterns 　Declarative 　Imperative 　Interrogative 　Exclamatory 　Simple 　Compound 　Complex 　Compound-Complex 　Loose/Cumulative 　Periodic 　Balanced 　Inversion 　Interruption 　Juxtaposition 　Parallelism 　Repetition	• *Punctuation:* How does the author punctuate the sentence, and to what extent does the punctuation affect the meaning? • *Structure:* How are words and phrases arranged within the sentence? What is the author trying to accomplish through this arrangement? • How would you characterize the author's syntax in this text? • *Changes:* Are there places where the syntax clearly changes? If so, where, how, and why? • *Sentence length:* How many words are in the different sentences? Do you notice any pattern (e.g., a cluster of short sentences of a particular type)? • *Devices:* How would you describe the author's use of the following: 　• Independent and dependent clauses 　• Coordinating, subordinating, or correlative conjunctions 　• Repetition 　• Parallelism 　• Fragments 　• Comparisons • *Sentence beginnings:* How does the author begin his or her sentences? (Does the author, for example, consistently begin with introductory phrases or clauses?) • *Language:* What use does the author make of figurative language or colloquial expressions?
Attitude (Tone) Word choice Details Imagery	• How does the author's use of words, details, or imagery, such as gesture or allusions, reveal the author's attitude toward a character or event in the story? • What words best describe the author's attitude toward this subject, character, or event?
Literary Elements Setting Characterization Plot Theme Point of View Tone/Attitude	• How does the author's use of these different elements contribute to the text's meaning? • Do the different elements interact with or otherwise affect the meaning of other elements? • Do you notice any significant shifts in any of the elements at any point? If so, what changes, and how and why? What is the importance and meaning of this change? • What words best describe the different use of these elements? For example, how would you describe the point of view and the effect it has on the meaning of the text?
Organization Compare/Contrast Importance Chronology Cause-Effect Order of Degree Classification Spatial	• Which organizational pattern does the author use? • Why does the author choose to use that particular organizational strategy? • Are there places where the author blends or alternates between different organizational patterns? If so, what is the author trying to accomplish by mixing them in these ways? • To what extent and in what ways do you think the author's organizational strategy is effective? Why?
Types of Writing Narrative Persuasive Expository Descriptive	• *Exposition:* Is the author defining, comparing, classifying, analyzing (a process), describing, or narrating? • *Persuasion:* Is the author arguing about what something means, whether something is true, which alternative is the best (or most important), or what course of action someone should take? • *General:* What is the author trying to accomplish? How is the writer using, for example, narrative writing to solve that problem?

▶ Summary Exemplar

In "Understanding Phobias," the author explains what a phobia is and how it can disrupt a person's daily life. While fear is natural, a phobia causes "overwhelming fear" that prevents people from living their lives. Phobias, which are among the most common mental illnesses, fall into four categories. Agoraphobics avoid situations from which they fear they cannot escape or get help. In the most extreme cases, people with agoraphobia will not leave their home. Another type of phobia focuses on social situations. Victims of "social phobias" are terrified of being publicly humiliated. Situations that make them feel watched—speaking before a group or, in some cases, even ordering food in a restaurant—cause a feeling of dread, so they try to avoid such situations. The other phobia involves a specific object or situation. These "specific phobias" often develop in childhood. For example, victims of social phobias might have an irrational fear of dogs or snakes, flying, or heights. The good news is that specific phobias are often the most easily treated; often people simply outgrow them as they age and realize that the dark is nothing to fear and that there are, in fact, no monsters under their bed.

In "Understanding Phobias," the author outlines different types of phobias and how they can be treated. The first group, agoraphobics, avoid situations from which they fear they cannot escape or get help. In the most extreme cases, people with agoraphobia will not leave their home. **Another type of phobia focuses on social situations.** Victims of "social phobias" are terrified of being publicly humiliated. Situations that make them feel watched—speaking before a group or, in some cases, even ordering food in a restaurant—cause a feeling of dread, so they try to avoid such situations. **The other phobia involves a specific object or situation.** These "specific phobias" often develop in childhood. For example, victims of social phobias might have an irrational fear of dogs or snakes, flying, or heights. **The good news is that phobias can be treated.** Some, such as fear of the dark, people simply outgrow. Other phobias are more complex and may require a combination of therapy and even anti-anxiety medications to help them overcome their fears.

Name: _____ Period: _____ Date: _____

◖ Summary Notes

Subject: _____

© 2007 by Jim Burke from *50 Essential Lessons* (Portsmouth, NH: Heinemann). This page may be reproduced for classroom use only.

BEFORE

1. Determine your purpose.
2. Preview the document.
3. Prepare to take notes.

DURING

4. Take notes to help you answer these questions:
   - Who is involved?
   - What events, ideas, or people does the author emphasize?
   - What are the causes?
   - What are the consequences or implications?
5. Establish criteria to determine what is important enough to include in the summary.
6. Evaluate information as you read to determine if it meets your criteria for importance.

AFTER

7. Write your summary, which should:
   - Identify the title, author, and topic in the first sentence.
   - State the main idea in the second sentence.
   - Be shorter than the original article
   - Begin with a sentence that states the topic (see sample).
   - Include a second sentence that states the author's main idea.
   - Include 3–5 sentences in which you explain—in your own words—the author's point of view.
   - Include one or two interesting quotations or details.
   - Maintain the author's meaning
   - Organize the ideas in the order in which they appear in the article.
   - Use transitions such as "according to" and the author's name to show that you are summarizing someone else's ideas.
   - Include enough information so that someone who has not read the article will understand the ideas.

Sample verbs: The author:

- argues
- asserts
- concludes
- considers
- discusses
- emphasizes
- examines
- explores
- focuses on
- implies
- mentions
- notes
- points out
- says
- states
- suggests

Sample summary written by a student

In "Surviving a Year of Sleepless Nights," Jenny Hung discusses *success and how it may not be so good.* Hung points out that *having fun is better than having success and glory.* Jenny Hung survived a painful year because of having too many honors classes, getting straight A's, and having a GPA of 4.43. Why would any of this be bad? It's because she wasn't happy. She describes working so hard for something she didn't really want. At one point she says, "There was even a month in winter when I was so self-conscious of my raccoon eyes that I wore sunglasses to school." She says she often stayed up late doing work and studying for tests for her classes. After what she had been through, she decided that it was not her life and chose her classes carefully once sophomore year came around.

Name: _____ Period: _____ Date: _____

▶ Summary of Basic Questions

Questions About Motives

1. ACT. What does the character do?

2. SITUATION. How does the character understand the situation in which she acts?

3. AGENT:

   (a) MORAL CHARACTER. What is the character's general moral character (disposition, temperament, values, habits, beliefs, sentiments, and so on)?

   (b) SELF-UNDERSTANDING. How does the character understand herself as the agent of this act?

4. PURPOSE. What does the character intend—aim to gain or accomplish—by this act?

5. ATTITUDE. With what feelings, in what manner, does the character perform this act (for example, eagerly or reluctantly)?

Questions About Any Work

A. What goes with what? (Identification; Association)

B. What versus what? (Contrast; Opposition; Conflict)

C. What follows what? (Progression; Sequence)

D. What becomes what? (Change; Transformation)

Examples: What has this character learned? How are things different at the end of the work than they were at the beginning?

Evaluative Questions

TRUTH. *Examples:* Is this character's understanding of her situation true or false, and why? In what ways is it true (accurate, adequate, valid), and why? In what ways is it false (inaccurate, inadequate, invalid), and why?

GOODNESS. (a) MORAL CHARACTER. *Examples:* Is this character a good person or a bad one, and why? In what ways is this character a good person, and why? In what ways is she a bad one, and why? (b) ACT. Is this act good or bad, and why? In what ways is this act good, and why? In what ways is it bad, and why?

Consider (1) the agent's purposes (or intentions): Are her purposes good or bad, and why? In what ways are her purposes good, and why? In what ways are they bad, and why?

Consider also (2) the consequences of the act: Are the consequences of this act good or bad, and why? In what ways are the consequences good, and why? In what ways are they bad, and why? Should the character be praised for these good consequences? Why or why not? Should she be blamed for these bad ones? Why or Why not?

Reprinted with permission from *Thinking About Literature* by Robert McMahon. © 2003 by Robert McMahon. Published by Heinemann, a division of Reed Elsevier, Inc., Portsmouth, NH. All rights reserved.

Summary Response Notes

1. **Write the title and author of the article here:**

   _____

   _____

2. **Set a purpose: What are you trying to answer about this subject?**

   _____

   _____

   _____

   _____

3. **Preview the article: Jot down three things you know based on your preview:**

   a. _____

   _____

   b. _____

   _____

   c. _____

   _____

4. **Read the article. Then write a summary (on the back or a separate piece of paper).**
   Model your summary on the following student example:

   In "Surviving a Year of Sleepless Nights," Jenny Hung **discusses** <u>success and how it may not be so good</u>. Hung **points out** <u>that having fun is better than having success and glory</u>. Jenny Hung survived a painful year because of having too many honors classes, getting straight A's, and having a GPA of 4.43. Why would any of this be bad? It's because she wasn't happy. She describes working so hard for something she didn't really want. **At one point she says**, "There was even a month in winter when I was so self-conscious of my raccoon eyes that I wore sunglasses to school." She says she often stayed up late doing work and studying for tests for her classes. After what she had been through, she decided that it was not her life and chose her classes carefully once sophomore year came around.

5. **Develop a discussion question based on your reading.** Write your question below, and be prepared to present it to the group as part of our discussion. It cannot be a yes/no question, nor can it be a question whose answer is a simple fact. The purpose of the question is to engage us in a thoughtful discussion.

   Example: Why would someone kill Martin Luther King, Jr., or Mahatma Gandhi?

   _____

   _____

   _____

   _____

Name: _____ Period: _____ Date: _____

◖ Target Notes

Subject: _____

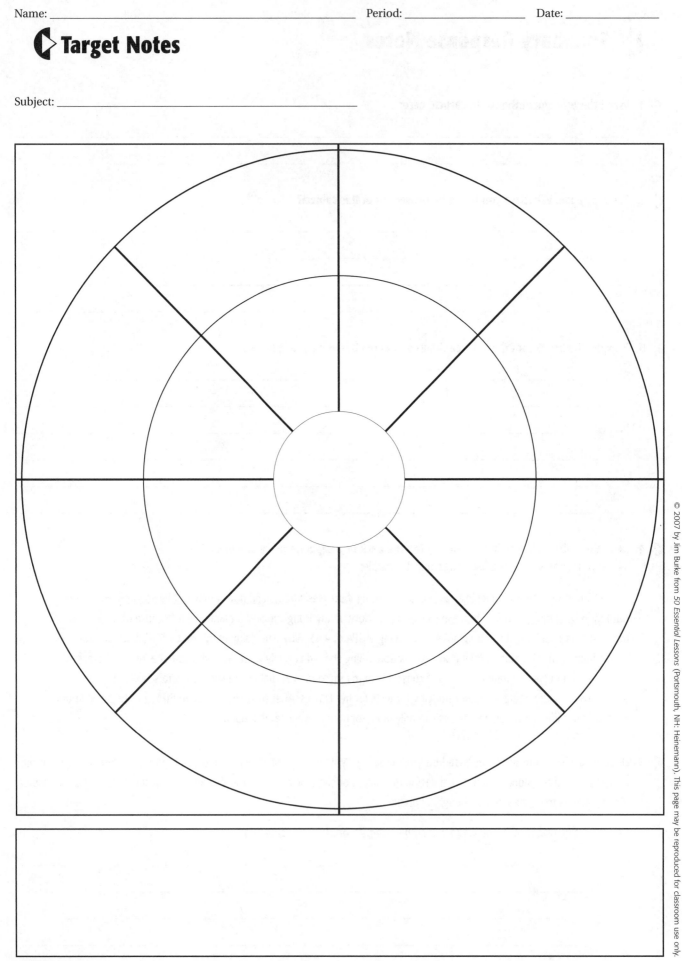

◖ Teaching Note-Taking Skills: Overview

◖ What It Is

Note taking includes a range of formats and functions. In short, it means reading, writing, listening, viewing, or observing with a pencil in hand so students can capture their thoughts and prepare for subsequent writing assignments, discussions, or exams. Note taking includes graphic formats and marginal comments, as well as more traditional methods like outlines, lists, and Cornell Notes. Highlighting and underlining are not the same as taking notes; while readers "take note" of some idea or change when they highlight, they are not thoroughly processing the information the way they would if they annotated the same passage.

◖ Why Use It

Taking notes demands that the students interact with the material and process it, making connections, evaluating importance, and organizing ideas into patterns that will not only prepare them for subsequent assignments but help them achieve deeper understanding of the material. Taking notes gives the students purpose and a process that ideally allows the students to use their own cognitive style and talents.

◖ When to Use It

Have students take notes whenever they must make sense of and remember (so that they can later use) whatever they read, watch, hear, or observe. When students give presentations in class, they pay better attention (and behave better) when they have to take notes on each student's presentation; it also improves their listening skills, which are essential for success in college and the workplace.

◖ How to Do It

The four formats listed below offer a range of styles. Which one students use depends on their purpose and preferences.

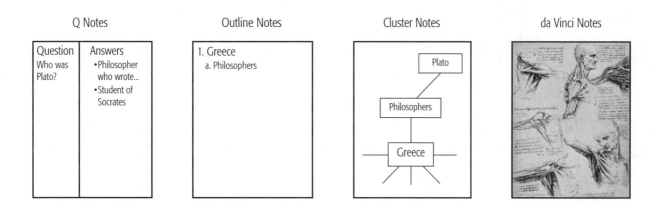

Q Notes — Outline Notes — Cluster Notes — da Vinci Notes

◖ See the companion page, "Making Effective and Efficient Notes," for more suggestions.

Consider these additional techniques for teaching and using note taking in your class:

- Model on the overhead (or by providing a sample on paper) how to take notes about a given text. If, for example, you ask students to take notes on a video, show them what that looks like, discuss which questions to ask, and help them format their notes.
- Put examples of exemplary notes (e.g., for reading the course textbook) on the overhead and give copies to everyone so they can refer to those examples when they do their reading. This is especially useful if some students use unique methods (e.g., color coding, graphic strategies, or the computer) in powerful ways.
- BDA: Remind them Before, During, and After that they should do certain things. Before beginning, for example, they should set a purpose, establish criteria for what to write down, and decide on the format that will be best suited to their purpose. During, they should note key terms and leave space to add material (or sample text questions) later. After, they should supplement their notes from additional reading and lectures to prepare for the test.

◖ Now Try It! Have students read the assigned text and use the method that seems most appropriate to the task.

▷ Test Creator

Question Type	Example	Notes
Vocabulary	Which of the following best defines *resolute* in the sentence, "The President was *resolute* in his efforts to…"	• Word • Defined • Explained
Factual	How long did the Wright brothers' first plane stay in the air?	Find the answer *in* the text, *on* the page.
Analytical	How—and why—does the character change by the end of the story?	Find the answer *between the lines*; make an inference.
Essay	Agree or disagree: Choose one invention from the Industrial Revolution that continues to benefit us today. Discuss three ways in which this invention has made life easier or better for people. Be sure to provide examples.	Draw from source to illustrate and support what you are saying about the subject.

Question Type	Factual
Question	Why did George and Lenny leave their last job?
Answer	Because Lenny was accused of raping a woman so they had to get out of town.
Evaluate (1–10)	10
Explain	This is a *very* important question because it gives us essential information about both men and foreshadows later events in the story.

Question Type	
Question	
Answer	
Evaluate (1–10)	
Explain	

Test Question Creator

Name: _____ Period: _____ Date: _____

Question	Answer	Importance
Example: What three continents join together to form the Arabian Peninsula?	Africa, Europe, and Asia	It's important because this served as perhaps the most important crossroads in the ancient world. People traded not only food but languages, customs, and cultures.

◖ Test-Maker Tool

Book Title _____

_____ **Vocabulary**

- Word
- Defined
- Explained

☐ Challenging
☐ Relevant
☐ Unimportant

Sample Words: valiant, pessimistic, legitimate, persevere, bureaucratic, memoir

Sample Question: which of the following best defines _____ as it is used in this sentence...

_____

_____

_____

_____

_____ **Factual**
Question & Answer

- Find the answer *in the text.*

☐ Important
☐ Useful
☐ Irrelevant

Example: How long did the Wright brothers' first plane stay in the air?

_____

_____

_____

_____

_____

_____ **Analytical**
Question & Answer

- Find the answer *between the lines.*

☐ Insightful
☐ Useful
☐ Unimportant

Example: How—and why—does the character change by the end of the story? Provide examples.

_____

_____

_____

_____

_____

_____ **Essay**
Question & Response

- Write one paragraph.
- Establish main idea for the paragraph.
- Develop your paragraph with supporting details/examples.
- Make sure your writing flows from one idea to the next.

☐ Challenging
☐ Interesting
☐ Superficial

Example: Agree or disagree: Socrates was guilty. Support your claim with specific examples from the readings.

_____

_____

_____

_____

_____

_____

_____

_____

◖ Test-Taking Strategy Directions

Use these directions to *practice* taking tests that require you to read a passage and answer multiple-choice questions. In actual test situations, you may not be allowed to write on the test. Don't make any stray marks on answer sheets for a computer-scored test.

1. Set a purpose: Turn the title (e.g., "Matter") into a PQ: What *is* matter?

2. Preview the text: Skim the heading, the first line of each paragraph, and the questions (but not the answers).

3. Read the passage: Read carefully and underline key ideas.

4. Make a plan: Use these strategies for each question:

 a. Underline key words in the question.

 b. Use POE (Process of Elimination) to cross off incorrect responses.

 c. Put a dot (•) next to *possible* answers.

 d. Draw a line from the correct answer to the words in the text that provide evidence for your answer.

 e. Mark the correct answer.

5. Trade and grade!

6. Pause and reflect: Write your thoughts in the space below or on the back.

 a. How did you do?

 b. What went well?

 c. What went wrong?

 d. How can you do better next time?

Name: _____ Period: _____ Date: _____

▷ Text Tool

▷ **The Subject:** _____

▷ **The Question:** _____

▷ **Connections:**   Themes   Diction   Plot   Imagery   Tone

▷ **Notes and Quotes Toward an Answer:**   Page #

_____
_____
_____
_____
_____
_____
_____
_____
_____
_____
_____
_____
_____
_____
_____
_____
_____
_____
_____
_____
_____
_____
_____

▷ **The Answer (as a Claim) to the Question:**   Page #

_____
_____
_____
_____
_____
_____
_____

Name: _____ Period: _____ Date: _____

Textbook Feature Analysis
(page 1)

Textbook Title: _____

DIRECTIONS　　Use this activity to better understand the textbook for your most difficult class. Its purpose is to teach you how the textbook works by showing you what it includes and how these elements are organized.

Types of Text 1. Skim through the book and make a list of all the different types of documents or types of text you will have to read (include graphic texts like graphs and maps).	
Sidebars and Pull Boxes 2. Find examples of pull-out boxes or sidebars. What kind of information appears in these? Are they standardized throughout the book (e.g., "Profiles in History," "Science in the Workplace")?	
Feature: Typography 3. Find examples of different typefaces and styles. Write down the examples and where they appear (e.g., large, bold 24-point font for chapter titles and 18-point font for subheadings throughout the chapter). How does this book use bold-faced type? What does it mean when writers use *italicized* words?	
Feature: Color 4. Does the textbook use color to convey information? For example, what does it mean when you see words in red ink on the page?	
Feature: Symbols and Icons 5. Does the textbook use symbols or icons to convey information? For example, if you see an icon with a question mark in it, what does that mean? Are you supposed to do something, like ask a question? Does it mean this is a potential test question? Or is it a link to a theme running throughout the book?	
Features: Images and Graphics 6. What kind of information accompanies illustrations or images? Find examples of a map, a chart, and a photograph and then look for captions or sidebars that explain or discuss the image. How is the image identified (e.g., Figure 2.6)?	

Textbook Feature Analysis
(page 2)

Organization 7. How are chapters organized? Make a brief but accurate outline.	
Navigation: Headers and Footers 8. Look at the top and bottom of the pages of the book. These are called the headers and footers. What kind of information is contained in this space? What do you notice as you flip through fifty consecutive pages? (e.g., Does the content of the header or footer change? If so, in what way? For what purpose?)	
Testing! Testing! 9. Imagine you must now prepare for a big test. What features of this book would help you to prepare for that test? (Hint: Do not limit your answer to the practice or study questions.)	
Note-Making Strategies 10. Q Notes or Outline Notes would probably help you the most while reading this book. Read a page and create an example for yourself of what good notes for this book will look like. You could also use sticky notes to annotate your textbook since you cannot write in it.	
Reading Speed 11. While your teacher times you, read one page of the book, taking notes as you normally would while reading it for homework. How long did that take you? Now do the math: If your teacher tells you to read the opening section for tomorrow and this section is ten pages long, how much time do you need to allot for your homework in this class?	
Concerns 12. After familiarizing yourself with this textbook, you may have concerns or questions. Getting these answered up front might help you read the textbook with greater success and confidence. Take this time to list any concerns you might have (e.g., reading speed, vocabulary).	

© 2007 by Jim Burke from *50 Essential Lessons* (Portsmouth, NH: Heinemann). This page may be reproduced for classroom use only.

◗ Textbook Notes Exemplar

Continuum of Importance

◗ Before Reading
Generate a BQ based on a skim of the headers, front matter, or title.
(BQ = Big Question; could also lean more toward EQ = Essential Question)

What was the source of the Spanish empire's power, and how did that relate to European absolutism?

◗ During Reading
Generate a PQ based on headers

◗ Example
(should read like sample quiz/test questions)
What was the source of Spain's power under Phillip II?

- Phillip's aggressive ways and deep religious faith
  - Seized Portugal and its empire
- Great wealth from America, empire
- Military power: Wealth funded large army
- Religious faith: The church was very important to him
  - Defended the faith against the Ottoman empire
  - Fought (and lost to) England to "punish Protestants"

◗ During Reading
Respond

◗ Example
What is the source of power in our own country under President Bush?

I think our country is a lot like Spain at that time. They had a ton of money and so do we. That money gave them power to do things just like it does for us. Right now, for example, President Bush can have a big military and go to war in Iraq or help the people in LA because we have the money. He's also very religious; people always talk about how important President Bush's religious faith is to him.

◗ After Reading
Reflect and Review

Return to your PQ and turn it into a claim. Using your notes, develop your claim into a paragraph that is focused, organized (chronologically, cause-effect, compare-contrast, classification, or order of importance), and developed (with examples, quotations, details) and has purpose (to explain, persuade, define, compare-contrast, show cause and effect, or classify).

Name: _____ Period: _____ Date: _____

Theme Tool

Defining Theme

A theme:

- Is a "controlling" idea about life or human nature that unifies the story
- May be stated directly or, more often, implied throughout the story
- Cannot be expressed in a single word or as a cliché, lesson, or moral

A theme statement:

- Is a complete sentence that is not so general as to apply to everything but specific enough that it provides insight throughout the story
    - A phrase is *not* a full development of a theme: e.g., *being a phony*
    - A word is *not* a full development of a theme: e.g., *phony*
- Applies to every character, event, and detail of the story; that is, nothing in the story should contradict the theme statement

DIRECTIONS

Developing a Theme Statement

1. Generate a list of central subjects in the story.

2. Evaluate these subjects and choose the *one* that is most important and central to the story.

3. Create a theme statement about that subject, making sure it meets the criteria outlined above.

Subject

Example: *phony*

Theme Statement

- Early on in *The Catcher in the Rye,* Salinger establishes the idea that it's important not to be a "phony," even as the book details how difficult that struggle really is.

_____

_____

_____

_____

_____

_____

_____

_____

_____

_____

_____

_____

Weaving the Thematic Threads: Connecting Your Theme to the Text

What the Text Says	How It Connects to Theme	Page #

Continue on back.

90 Tools and Texts

© 2007 by Jim Burke from *50 Essential Lessons* (Portsmouth, NH: Heinemann). This page may be reproduced for classroom use only.

Name: _____ Period: _____ Date: _____

▷ Three-Column Organizer

◖ **Time Line Notes**

DIRECTIONS — Each line represents the next stage in a sequence. In a novel this might mean the next scene or chapter; in a historical text it might mean the next event or year. In the box underneath each line, explain why it happened, what it means, why it is important, or what it will cause to happen next.

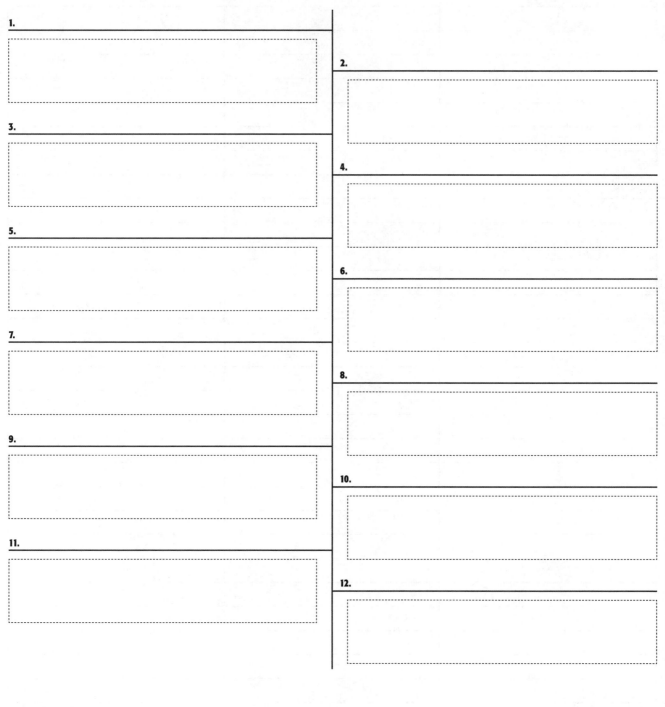

1.

2.

3.

4.

5.

6.

7.

8.

9.

10.

11.

12.

◖ **Notes/Observations**

▶ Traits that Contribute to Economic Success

DIRECTIONS   This list of traits associated with economic or financial success is compiled from multiple sources and arranged alphabetically. Arrange the factors in order of importance to you. Be prepared to explain your thinking.

Acting on opportunities

Being healthy

Being competitive

Being intelligent

Being honest

Being lucky

Being organized

Being prepared to take risks

Continually learning about your field

Enjoying your work

Focusing on financial goals

Getting good advice

Having a college degree

Having good communication skills

Having on-the-job experience

Having support from your spouse/family

Investing money to make more money

Knowing how to sell your product or skill

Making good decisions

Managing money wisely

Solving problems

Spending less money than you make

Understanding business and tax laws

Working harder than others

Working well with others

◖ Understanding Argument: An Overview

Adapted from *The Craft of Research*, 2nd Edition, by Booth, Colomb, and Williams. © 2003. Reprinted by permission of The University of Chicago Press.

Name: _____

Element	Question to Ask	Traits of Effective Argument	Example	Language
1. Make a *claim*. (Your proposition, or assertion; the central point you will argue. The "main claim" for a paper is also known as the "thesis.")	What do you ***claim?***	• not obvious • defendable • debatable • not a fact/opinion • significant • avoids either/or		• I think X because…. • X suggests Y since…. • Because X leads to Y, Z must happen. • A leads to B because C….
2. State your *reasons*. (Sentence or two that explain why readers should accept your claim.)	What ***reasons*** support that claim?	• logical • persuasive • relevant • substantial • appealing		• based on…. • According to A, B stems from…. • Studies consistently show that A leads to B…. • X found that Y caused Z when A happened. • A concluded B based on C. • X demonstrated that Y….
3. Provide *evidence* to support your claim. (Consists of facts, figures, or statistics used to prove the claim. Should be something that can be seen, touched, heard, felt, a *fact*.)	What ***evidence*** supports those reasons?	• Avoid logical fallacies. • Valid ***evidence*** is: • authoritative • relevant • specific • effective • current • compelling		
4. *Acknowledge and respond to* opposing perspectives. (A good claim challenges previously held beliefs. You must recognize the other points of view and then explain how your claim disproves or improves upon the other claims.)	Do you ***acknowledge*** this alternative/complication/objection—and how do you ***respond?***	• Use concessionary language to ***acknowledge*** and ***respond.*** • Cite specific important alternatives or objections, and then address them head on with reliable evidence to support your claim.		Use subordinating conjunctions (*although*, *as if*, *because*, *unless*, *while*, etc.) to signal concession, e.g., While X consistently shows Y, not everyone agrees with the results or the method by which these results are obtained.
5. *Ethos* (Invisible sixth element of any argument; relates to image of the author reflected in the claim and supporting details.)	What is the author's or speaker's ***ethos?*** How do we know we can believe what he or she says?	• Be thorough. • Establish and maintain credibility throughout. • Focus on quality of the argument's construction. • Consider integrity of sources.		What the writer/speaker does not want to do is use—or at least overuse—the pronoun *I*, as if to imply "if I say or think it, it must be true."

 **Video Notes**

Video title: _____

▷ **Before watching:** Jot down what you know, make predictions, write questions....Use the video title to develop a PQ (purpose question): _____

▷ **While watching:** Take notes that relate to your PQ. _____

▷ **After watching:** Write a summarizing paragraph. To do this, turn your PQ into a claim. Use your notes to support and illustrate your claim. _____

◗ Visualizing Strategies: Reading Is Seeing

◗ Use visualizing when:

❏ The text is difficult, in particular because it is abstract or hard to follow.

❏ You are struggling to see how the information or text is organized.

❏ The material is vague or foreign; lack of exposure or knowledge makes it hard to imagine what you are reading (e.g., ancient texts like Homer's *The Odyssey*).

❏ You want an alternative way to make sense of and respond to what you read, particularly using your spatial, visual abilities.

Draw the Text	Using the actual words from the text as your guidelines, translate the text into a drawing to help you see what it looks like and what is happening. **Example:** In Homer's *The Odyssey,* he describes the hall in which the suitors gather; yet it is so foreign to our experience. Draw the hall in precise detail, using each sentence in the section as a checklist of what to include, how to arrange it, and what it looks like.
Sensory Notes	Create a page with columns for the different senses (e.g., sounds, smells, etc.). As you read, write down any sensory details the text includes. When you have finished reading the selection, use those details to write a description of the scene that will show you understand what you read and help you see what it looks like and thus better visualize what you read. You can also use this list of details to analyze the author's style. **Example:** In *A Tale of Two Cities,* Dickens uses abundant sensory details to help readers see and sense what the London of his era was like and how its people lived and looked.
Visual Explanation	Use some sort of symbolic means of representing movement and connections. One possibility is to envision those complex diagrams football coaches draw to show who is going where and doing what on a given football play. **Example:** In *Julius Caesar,* Cassius is left standing alone at the end of Act One. Throughout the act, however, he is everywhere, talking to everyone. Using a set of dots somewhat like billiard balls that have an initial for each character in them (e.g., © for Cassius), show how Cassius moves through the act; then explain what it means that he stands alone at the end of the first act.
Perform the Text	Whether role playing a scene or creating a tableau to represent a moment, create a physical visible performance that corresponds with the text. **Example:** When reading *Lord of the Flies,* place everyone in formation to show the different dynamics in the opening scene as Jack enters, blinded by the sun, and towers over Ralph who is impressed by the boy "who knows his own mind."
Compare the Text	Comparing what you do not understand to what you do understand helps to create a visual sense of comparison. **Example:** Thus if you say, "Gatsby is like a grown-up Holden Caulfield," you might better understand the text.
Recast the Text	Recasting a written text into a movie script or even a poem can sometimes help you better understand it by thinking about it and working with it in a different, more visual genre. **Example:** Describe the battle scenes from Homer's *The Odyssey* as Speilberg would the opening scene for *Saving Private Ryan* of D-Day in WW II.

© 2007 by Jim Burke from *50 Essential Lessons* (Portsmouth, NH: Heinemann). This page may be reproduced for classroom use only.

Name: _____ Period: _____ Date: _____

Weekly Record

Set a Goal ("By Friday, I will...")

	PASE Yourself	
	Personal	**A**cademic
	Social	**E**xtracurricular

Make a Plan (List two specific actions or strategies that will help you reach this goal by Friday.)

1.

2.

Self-Evaluation (Describe *what* you accomplished, *why* you accomplished it, and *evidence* that you did.)

Weekly Wisdom (What did you learn about yourself, people, or the world this week–and how?)

Weekly Academic Record

	Class	Teacher	Homework Total	Done	Quizzes	Tests	Progress Report Grade	Absent	Late	Grade
1										
2										
3										
4										
5										
6										

Weekly Reflection

Suggestions/Prompts

- This week I finally...
- One strategy that helped was...
- I felt really good when I...
- I got very frustrated by...
- What worked/what did not...
- Last week I...but this week...
- It's hard for me to... because...
- What went well/what did not...
- What's hard/getting easier...

Name: _____ Period: _____ Date: _____

◖ Writing Effective Introductions

DIRECTIONS

Do each step listed below:

1. Read all four introductions, annotating what each does effectively.

2. Choose the one you think is most effective and explain why you think it is so compelling. Identify specific strategies the author uses in that paragraph.

3. Write a sample introduction (as if you were going to write an entire essay) about some aspect of your novel (e.g., moral character, author's use of dreams, recurring theme).

1. Ken Kesey's *One Flew Over the Cuckoo's Nest* explores the idea of oppression in modern society. Kesey uses the mental hospital as a metaphor for the oppression and intolerance that existed in America before the counterculture of the 1960s. Randle McMurphy is the story's protagonist, and he embodies all of the elements of a rebel. McMurphy is a jovial man whose laughter symbolizes specific changes throughout the novel.

2. *The Plague* argues fervently for Camus's existential humanism. From the beginning, we are shown humanity's struggle with death, and we look on as people become aware of their lives and have to fight to make something of them. Oran, the city that will eventually be struck by plague, is described initially as "a city without pigeons, without trees or gardens" (1). It is a lifeless place, desolate and ugly, and so "everyone is bored" (4). The people living in the town pay no attention to each other, and go about their business mechanically and pointlessly, trying to make money before they die. They live in a state of undeath, not truly alive, but still moving around.

3. Fyodor Dostoevski wrote in 1866 that "humans can get used to anything." Almost a hundred years later, Alexander Solzhenitsyn wrote *A Day in the Life of Ivan Denisovich*, a novel based on his experiences in a Stalin-era gulag, which supports Dostoevski's statement. In it, Shukhov (called Ivan Denisovich by others) ekes out a bearable existence despite the draconian rigors of his imprisonment. With this simple premise, Solzhenitsyn explores the relative nature of happiness in *A Day in the Life of Ivan Denisovich* by creating a character who contents himself even in the harshest of circumstances.

4. Faulkner's novel *As I Lay Dying* illustrates the unraveling of a family after the death of Addie Brunden, a mother and wife. Faulkner utilizes a series of short chapters told in first person by all different characters to let the audience know the inner thoughts of these characters. The audience learns about Cash as well through his narrations, but Jewel remains a mystery. Cash's carpentry, as portrayed in the first chapter, symbolizes his steady character, while Jewel's actions in the beginning of the novel represent his independence and his separation from the rest of the family.

© 2007 by Jim Burke from *50 Essential Lessons* (Portsmouth, NH: Heinemann). This page may be reproduced for classroom use only.

BURP, RUMBLE, TOOT!

How your lunch can turn you into a one-person band

BY KAREN BARROW

Y ou gulp a can of soda, and a few minutes later. . . BURP! You feel hungry, and hear a noise from your stomach. . . GRUMBLE! You eat cafeteria's spicy bean dip, . . . well, you know what happens.

"You may laugh, but everyone's body makes noise," says David Sachar, a *gastroenterologist*, or doctor of the stomach and intestines, at Mount Sinai School of Medicine in New York City.

And even though your body's orchestra may make funny sounds, the noise is a sign that your *gastrointestinal system* (body system that breaks down food for use) is doing its job— digesting food and getting rid of waste. That's because behind all the rumbles and toots is one ingredient your body doesn't need: gas.

Let's take a tour of your insides to find out where all the gas comes from, and why it leaves in such noisy ways.

EATING AIR

It's lunchtime. You and your friends are munching on sandwiches and

chips, laughing about the corny joke your science teacher told today. But along with the turkey on rye, something else is sliding down your throat that will exit later as a gassy burst: "Burps are mostly swallowed air," says Sachar.

Drinking bubbly drinks, talking, chewing gum, and eating too quickly can cause you to swallow a lot of air. That air gets pushed down your *esophagus* (eh-SAH-fah-gus), a tube that connects your throat to your stomach. The air fills your stomach and, soon, there's no room left in your blown-up

Tools and Texts 99

BURP, RUMBLE, TOOT! (page 2)

tummy. How to get rid of the air? Some of it gets squeezed back out of your mouth, using *eructation* (ih-rehk-TAY-shun), a fancy word for burping.

No matter how hard you may try, it's tough to muffle the noise. That's because when you eat, a tiny flap of tissue, called the *epiglottis* (eh-pih-GLAH-tis), flops over to cover your windpipe and prevent swallowed food from traveling into your lungs. Between bites, the tissue flops back over your esophagus to let you breathe. As a burp is born, the air pushes past the epiglottis. This causes the flap to vibrate and move the air in your throat, creating *sound waves*. These vibrating energy waves give a burp its noisy blast.

Even if you avoid soda and put the gum away, the occasional burp will surely still slip by. Just be sure to cover your mouth to be polite.

RUMBLE IN YOUR TUMMY

Lunch was great, but by the time 3 p.m. hits, all you can think about is an after-school snack. You hear a grumble from below reminding you that it's time to eat. Turns out, those gurgles don't really come from your stomach.

Inside your stomach, chemicals called *enzymes* break down your food into its smallest parts, called *nutrients*. These enzymes can't completely digest all your food. So after about four hours of sitting in your stomach, the leftover, partially digested mush moves on to the *small intestine*, where even more digestion will take place.

The small intestine is a snaking, narrow tube roughly 6 meters (20 feet) long. To shuttle the mush through this tube, muscles around the intestine ripple with wavelike contractions, called *peristalsis* (per-eh-STAHL-sehs). As the slushy food and leftover gas squish through the intestines, you may hear grumbles called *borborygmi* (bor-buh-RIG-my).

Even if your intestines are talking, you don't need to grab a snack right away. The gurgles and grumbles are just signals that your stomach has emptied enough to make room for the next meal. "It is just your body telling you that it's ready for food," says Sachar.

A MIGHTY WIND

So far, the sounds of gas have been echoing throughout your digestive system. But there's more to come!

Inside your *large intestine* are trillions of *microbes*. For these tiny organisms, the leftover food that survived the trip through your stomach and small intestine is an all-you-can-eat buffet. The microbes contain specialized enzymes that

are able to break down and digest the remaining food. They *metabolize* some of the nutrients, converting them into the energy they need to grow.

However, as the microbes feast, they produce waste in the form of—you guessed it—gas. The gas builds up and pushes through the rest of your intestine. Then, out of your body it goes—toot!

MEGABLAST

Foods like beans, broccoli, and milk products are especially hard for your stomach and small intestine to digest. That's because they are made of tough sugar *molecules*, or particles of two or more atoms joined together. Foods with these compounds make it to your large intestine without breaking down much.

So when you eat a bean burrito topped with extra cheese, the microbes get a supersize meal. The extra gas they produce powers through your large intestine, causing more *flatulence* (FLA-chuh-lense) than usual. "The stronger the wind, the louder the result," says Alan Baird, a *physiologist* (scientist who studies the body's vital functions) at the University College Dublin in Ireland.

The gas you blast is a combination of nitrogen, oxygen, carbon dioxide, hydrogen, and methane—the same gases that make up the air you breathe. So why does your released gas sometimes smell? When certain types of foods are digested, they produce a tiny amount of hydrogen sulfide, the same gas that gives rotten eggs their stinky scent.

PARDON ME

There is very little you can do to prevent gas. No matter what, you will pass gas approximately 14 times a day. And you'll burp a couple of times too.

Yes, body noises can be embarrassing. But your gastrointestinal system can't function without them. Just be sure that when a little gas does sneak past, you say, "excuse me." Then, thank your body for a job well done!

Could it be that video games are good for kids?

By Steven Johnson

"Could it be that video games are good for kids?" by Steve Johnson, reprinted in *San Francisco Chronicle*, July 29, 2005 (originally appeared in *Los Angeles Times*). Reprinted by permission of the author, via Paradigm.

Dear Sen. Clinton: I'm writing to commend you for calling for a $90-million study on the effects of video games on children, and in particular the courageous stand you have taken in recent weeks against the notorious "Grand Theft Auto" series.

I'd like to draw your attention to another game whose nonstop violence and hostility have captured the attention of millions of kids—a game that instills aggressive thoughts in the minds of its players, some of whom have gone on to commit real-world acts of violence and sexual assault after playing.

I'm talking, of course, about high school football.

I know a congressional investigation into football won't play so well with those crucial swing voters, but it makes about as much sense as an investigation into the pressing issue of Xbox and PlayStation 2.

Your current concern is over explicit sex in "Grand Theft Auto: San Andreas." Yet there's not much to investigate, is there? It should get rated appropriately, and that's that. But there's more to your proposed study: You want to examine how video games shape children's values and cognitive development.

Kids have always played games. A hundred years ago they were playing stickball and kick the can; now they're playing "World of Warcraft," "Halo 2" and "Madden 2005." And parents have to drag their kids away from the games to get them to do their algebra homework, but parents have been dragging kids away from whatever the kids were into since the dawn of civilization.

So any sensible investigation into video games must ask the "compared to what" question. If the alternative to playing "Halo 2" is reading "The Portrait of a Lady,"

Today's games force children to learn skills they'll need in the digital workforce.

then of course "The Portrait of a Lady" is better for you. But it's not as though kids have been reading Henry James for 100 years and then suddenly dropped him for Pokemon.

Another key question: Of all the games that kids play, which ones require the most mental exertion? Parents can play this at home: Try a few rounds of Monopoly or Go Fish with your kids, and see who wins. I suspect most families will find that it's a relatively even match. Then sit down and try to play "Halo 2" with the kids. You'll be lucky if you survive 10 minutes.

The great secret of today's video games that has been lost in the moral panic over "Grand Theft Auto" is how difficult the games have become. That difficulty is not merely a question of hand-to-eye coordination; most of today's games force kids to learn complex rule systems, master challenging new interfaces, follow dozens of shifting variables in real time and prioritize between multiple objectives.

In short, precisely the sorts of skills that they're going to need in the digital workplace of tomorrow.

Consider this one fascinating trend among teenagers: They're spending less time watching professional sports and more time simulating those sports on Xbox or PlayStation. Now, which activity challenges the mind more—sitting around rooting for the Green Bay Packers, or managing an entire football franchise through a season of "Madden 2005": calling plays, setting lineups, trading players and negotiating contracts? Which challenges the mind more—zoning out to the lives of fictional characters on a televised soap opera, or actively managing the lives of dozens of virtual characters in a game such as "The Sims"?

On to the issue of aggression, and what causes it in kids, especially teenage boys. Congress should be interested in the facts: The last 10 years have seen the

Could it be that video games are good for kids? (page 2)

release of many popular violent games, including "Quake" and "Grand Theft Auto"; that period also has seen the most dramatic drop in violent crime in recent memory. According to Duke University's Child Well-Being Index, today's kids are less violent than kids have been at any time since the study began in 1975. Perhaps, Sen. Clinton, your investigation should explore the theory that violent games function as a safety valve, letting children explore their natural aggression without acting it out in the real world.

Many juvenile crimes—such as the carjacking that is so central to "Grand Theft Auto"—are conventionally described as "thrill-seeking" crimes. Isn't it possible that kids no longer need real-world environments to get those thrills, now that the games simulate them so vividly? The national carjacking rate has dropped substantially since "Grand Theft Auto" came out. Isn't it conceivable that the would-be carjackers are now getting their thrills on the screen instead of the street?

Crime statistics are not the only sign that today's gaming generation is doing much better than the generation raised during the last cultural panic—over rock 'n' roll. Math SAT scores have never been higher; verbal scores have been climbing steadily for the last five years; nearly every indicator in the Department of Education study known as the Nation's Report Card is higher now than when the study was implemented in 1971.

By almost every measure, the kids are all right.

Of course, I admit that one charge against video games is a slam dunk. Kids don't get physical exercise when they play a video game, and indeed the rise in obesity among younger people is a serious issue. But, of course, you don't get exercise from doing homework, either.

Steven Johnson is author of Everything Bad Is Good for You: How Today's Popular Culture Is Actually Making Us Smarter *(Riverhead Hardcover, 2005). This commentary appeared originally in the* Los Angeles Times.

Dulce et Decorum Est
Wilfred Owen

Bent double, like old beggars under sacks,
Knock-kneed, coughing like hags, we cursed through sludge,
Till on the haunting flares we turned our backs
And towards our distant rest began to trudge.
Men marched asleep. Many had lost their boots
But limped on, blood-shod. All went lame; all blind;
Drunk with fatigue; deaf even to the hoots
Of tired, outstripped Five-Nines that dropped behind.

Gas! Gas! Quick, boys!—An ecstasy of fumbling,
Fitting the clumsy helmets just in time;
But someone still was yelling out and stumbling
And flound'ring like a man in fire or lime . . .
As under a green sea, I saw him drowning.
In all my dreams, before my helpless sight,
He plunges at me, guttering, choking, drowning.

If in some smothering dreams you too could pace
Behind the wagon that we flung him in,
And watch the white eyes writhing in his face,
His hanging face, like a devil's sick of sin;
If you could hear, at every jolt, the blood
Come gargling from the froth-corrupted lungs,
Obscene as cancer, bitter as the cud
Of vile, incurable sores on innocent tongues,—
My friend, you would not tell with such high zest
To children ardent for some desperate glory,
The old Lie: Dulce et decorum est
Pro patria mori.

Emmanuel Yeboah preps for Fitness Triathlon

MINNEAPOLIS - Born with a severely deformed leg in a country where the handicapped are considered a curse, Emmanuel Ofosu Yeboah was determined to show the people of Ghana that those with disabilities are capable of great things. So he jumped on a bicycle and started an improbable, Forrest Gump-like journey across his nation to prove just that.

"I see how people are treated in Ghana, and that's why I am giving all my effort to this," said the 28-year-old man, who was born without a shin bone. "I don't want to give up. I don't want to give up."

Yeboah's goal has now gone global.

He was in California this week to receive one of cable network ESPN's ESPY awards, an honor given to courageous athletes that's named after the late tennis star Arthur Ashe. Then he traveled to Minnesota to prepare for Saturday's Life Time Fitness Triathlon—where he will be responsible for the 25-mile bike portion of the race for a relay team participating in the event.

"It's been very good for me to come here," Yeboah said. "The people in Ghana, they can see how famous I am in the States. So many people there are very appreciative of what I am doing."

The details of this story, revealed through a soon-to-be-released documentary film about his life, *Emmanuel's Gift,* and a recent phone interview with Yeboah, are nothing short of fascinating.

Ghana, a nation of about 20 million people on the continent's west coast, is considered one of Africa's most enlightened countries as the first to establish its independence and a democratic government. But disabled people account for approximately 10 percent of the population, and they are generally shunned from society and resigned to a life of begging on the streets.

Yeboah was born without the lower part of his right leg, with a normal-sized foot essentially dangling from his thigh instead of a knee.

Because of the disability, his mother, Comfort, was advised to either kill him or leave him in the forest to die. Because of the disability, his father, Dickson, abandoned the family. But Yeboah refused to accept such a cruel fate.

"His mission is to change perceptions. He's the epitome of doing what you can with limited resources," said Bob Babbit, a co-founder of the California-based Challenged Athletes Foundation, which provided Yeboah with the bicycle that jump-started his quest three years ago.

Yeboah was making about $2 per day shining shoes, trying to provide a living for him and his family members, when he learned about CAF's grant program through a missionary in town. Praying to God while he wrote his first letter to America, Yeboah asked for a bike he could ride across the country—more than 370 miles to disprove the stereotype about the disabled.

After getting the hang of this awkward activity—basically pedaling with his healthy leg while his right foot rested on the frame—Yeboah secured enough sponsors to begin his ride. Skepticism hounded him, but the publicity picked up as people began to realize he was serious—and successful. Wearing a red, yellow and blue striped shirt, Yeboah rolled through village after village as wide-eyed children chased behind in awe and celebration.

The foundation later invited him to the San Diego area for its annual 56-mile bike ride in November 2002, his first trip outside of Ghana. Soon after, in April 2003, he was fitted with a prosthetic right leg. The next year, he shaved three hours off his time in the same event.

These accomplishments have been big enough in their own right, but Yeboah is not keen on stopping. He has people to take care of back home. One project on the horizon is the organization of a wheelchair basketball team that will represent Ghana at the 2008 Paralympic Games in Beijing.

"I believe that if it's not coming from your heart, you give up," Yeboah said. "But this is coming from your heart. You never give up."

Another part of his mission is to secure governmental regulations that will protect the rights of the disabled, something that's commonplace in the United States but unprecedented in Ghana.

"I believe that I'm not going to end it here," Yeboah said. "I'm going to continue until the time that I will die."

"Ghana Man Preps for Fitness Triathlon" by Dave Campbell, AP, July 16, 2005. Reprinted by permission of Associated Press via Reprint Management Services.

Facing It
Yusef Komunyakaa

My black face fades,
hiding inside the black granite.
I said I wouldn't,
dammit: No tears.
I'm stone. I'm flesh.
My clouded reflection eyes me
like a bird of prey, the profile of night
slanted against morning. I turn
this way—the stone lets me go.
I turn that way—I'm inside
the Vietnam Veterans Memorial
again, depending on the light
to make a difference.
I go down the 58,022 names,
half-expecting to find
my own in letters like smoke.
I touch the name Andrew Johnson;
I see the booby trap's white flash.
Names shimmer on a woman's blouse
but when she walks away
the names stay on the wall.
Brushstrokes flash, a red bird's
wings cutting across my stare.
The sky. A plane in the sky.
A white vet's image floats
closer to me, then his pale eyes
look through mine. I'm a window.
He's lost his right arm
inside the stone. In the black mirror
a woman's trying to erase names:
No, she's brushing a boy's hair.

"Facing It" by Yusef Komunyakaa from *Dien Cai Dau* (Wesleyan University Press, 1988), © 1988 by Yusef Komunyakaa and reprinted by permission of Wesleyan University Press.

Find and Focus

By Herm Edwards,
From *You Play to Win the Game*

Identify your goal and then create a plan. You've got to have a plan. If you don't have a plan, then you don't know which way to go.

When our season ends, the first thing I do is make a plan for the next one. I set my calendar, my schedule; I get the dates set from January to July so that everyone knows exactly what we're doing. I say, "Here's the dates; here's the plan. Here's where I want to go. January to July—bang—that's when training camp starts."

Now I can focus. I've got a start and a finish. Unless you understand where you're starting from and where you want to go, you can't get started. That's the hardest thing to do.

Remember when you got your first car? The first thing you did was look out the window every five minutes to make sure it was still there. You were sitting around with nowhere to go, hoping someone would call you to come over. You wanted to drive that car, so you would ask, "Mom, do you need something at the store?" You wanted to get in that car and go somewhere—you just needed a place to go.

It's the same thing when you're trying to accomplish something. There's a starting point. So now, where's the finishing point? You can't just start. You have to know where you're finishing, what's the end result. So you ask yourself, "Where am I trying to go?" "Well," you say, "I'm trying to go here—here's the start and here's the finish, here's where I want to go."

Once you have those, you're ready to draw the lines—the path you want to take to get from A to B, your plan for how you're going to get there. So you start making your plan, drawing the lines. But you don't draw them straight, because you're never going straight. That's not real life. You've got to allow for U-turns, reverses, left turns, right turns, ruts, speed bumps—all kinds of things that will present themselves as you go from A to B.

For example, say you're running a marathon. You know you've got a start, and you're pretty sure where the finish fine is. But you don't run a straight line to the finish. You might move to the side, grab some water, find a different group of people to run alongside, but you feel that finish line pulling you. You know where you're going, and it's drawing you closer.

It's the same thing with a goal. Say you want to lose 20 pounds and you give yourself six months to do it. Okay, that's a reasonable goal. You set a start date, you set an end date, and you map out what you're going to eat, when you're going to exercise, and how long you're going to exercise. You allow for a few U-turns, a few chocolate chip cookies or something, because you know you can't just eat salad for six months. But that's okay; you planned for it, so when it happens, it doesn't derail the whole thing. By the finish date, you've got the work done.

The day training camp starts in July, I know we've accomplished what we needed to do to start the next step. We've found our focus and the first part of our plan. Now we're ready to do it again. I tell my guys that having the ability to precisely define our goals and create a plan to achieve them shapes our entire attitude and the way we view life.

From *You Play to Win the Game: Leadership Lessons for Success On and Off the Field* by Herm Edwards, with Shelly Smith. Reprinted by permission of The McGraw-Hill Companies.

Genesis 3

The Fall

^{1}Now the serpent was more crafty than any other beast of the field that the LORD God had made.

He said to the woman, "Did God actually say, 'You shall not eat of any tree in the garden'?" ^{2}And the woman said to the serpent, "We may eat of the fruit of the trees in the garden, ^{3}but God said, 'You shall not eat of the fruit of the tree that is in the midst of the garden, neither shall you touch it, lest you die.'" ^{4}But the serpent said to the woman, "You will not surely die. ^{5}For God knows that when you eat of it your eyes will be opened, and you will be like God, knowing good and evil." ^{6}So when the woman saw that the tree was good for food, and that it was a delight to the eyes, and that the tree was to be desired to make one wise, she took of its fruit and ate, and she also gave some to her husband who was with her, and he ate. ^{7}Then the eyes of both were opened, and they knew that they were naked. And they sewed fig leaves together and made themselves loincloths.

^{8}And they heard the sound of the LORD God walking in the garden in the cool of the day, and the man and his wife hid themselves from the presence of the LORD God among the trees of the garden. ^{9}But the LORD God called to the man and said to him, "Where are you?" ^{10}And he said, "I heard the sound of you in the garden, and I was afraid, because I was naked, and I hid myself." ^{11}He said, "Who told you that you were naked? Have you eaten of the tree of which I commanded you not to eat?" ^{12}The man said, "The woman whom you gave to be with me, she gave me fruit of the tree, and I ate." ^{13}Then the LORD God said to the woman, "What is this that you have done?" The woman said, "The serpent deceived me, and I ate." ^{14}The LORD God said to the serpent, "Because you have done this, cursed are you above all livestock and above all beasts of the field; on your belly you shall go, and dust you shall eat all the days of your life. ^{15}I will put enmity between you and the woman, and between your offspring and her offspring; he shall bruise your head, and you shall bruise his heel."

^{16}To the woman he said, "I will surely multiply your pain in childbearing; in pain you shall bring forth children. Your desire shall be for your husband, and he shall rule over you." ^{17}And to Adam he said, "Because you have listened to the voice of your wife and have eaten of the tree of which I commanded you, 'You shall not eat of it,' cursed is the ground because of you; in pain you shall eat of it all the days of your life; ^{18}thorns and thistles it shall bring forth for you; and you shall eat the plants of the field. ^{19}By the sweat of your face you shall eat bread, till you return to the ground, for out of it you were taken; for you are dust, and to dust you shall return."

^{20}The man called his wife's name Eve, because she was the mother of all living. ^{21}And the LORD God made for Adam and for his wife garments of skins and clothed them. ^{22}Then the LORD God said, "Behold, the man has become like one of us in knowing good and evil. Now, lest he reach out his hand and take also of the tree of life and eat, and live forever—^{23}"therefore the LORD God sent him out from the garden of Eden to work the ground from which he was taken. ^{24}He drove out the man, and at the east of the garden of Eden he placed the cherubim and a flaming sword that turned every way to guard the way to the tree of life.

I Hear America Singing
Walt Whitman

I hear America singing, the varied carols I hear,
Those of mechanics, each one singing his as it should be blithe and strong,
The carpenter singing his as he measures his plank or beam,
The mason singing his as he makes ready for work, or leaves off work,
The boatman singing what belongs to him in his boat, the deckhand singing on the
    steamboat deck,
The shoemaker singing as he sits on his bench, the hatter singing as he stands,
The wood-cutter's song, the ploughboy's on his way in the morning, or at the noon
    intermission or at sundown,
The delicious singing of the mother, or of the young wife at work, or of the girl sewing
    or washing,
Each singing what belongs to him or her and to none else,
The day what belongs to the day—at night the party of young fellows, robust, friendly,
Singing with open mouths their strong melodious songs.

I, Too
Langston Hughes

I, too, sing America.

I am the darker brother.
They send me to eat in the kitchen
When company comes,
But I laugh,
And eat well,
And grow strong.

Tomorrow,
I'll be at the table
When company comes.
Nobody'll dare
Say to me,
"Eat in the kitchen,"
Then.

Besides,
They'll see how beautiful I am
And be ashamed—

I, too, am America.

"I, Too" from THE COLLECTED POEMS OF LANGSTON HUGHES by Langston Hughes, © 1994 by The Estate of Langston Hughes. Used by permission of Alfred A. Knopf, a division of Random House, Inc. and Harold Ober Associates.

INC. MAGAZINE: MOST FASCINATING ENTREPRENEURS:

—for simultaneously building a business and nurturing Latino culture

#26 Rueben Martinez *Libreria Martinez Books and Art Galleries*

By Jeffrey L. Seglin

Rueben Martinez is a genius, and he has the grant to prove it. Last year, he became the first bookseller to receive one of those $500,000 fellowships from the MacArthur Foundation that have come to be called "genius grants." The selection committee lauded Martinez for "fusing the roles of marketplace and community center to inspire appreciation of literature and preserve Latino literary heritage." All of that is certainly true, but that's not why we love Martinez. We love him because he exhibits the improvisational flair and versatility that are innate to master entrepreneurs.

Martinez's business, Libreria Martinez Books and Art Galleries, began its life as a small shelf in a barber shop in Santa Ana, Calif. For years, Martinez, a barber and the son of Mexican copper miners, lent copies of books like Juan Rulfo's *El Llano en llamas* to his customers. Eventually, he started selling books by Latino writers. By 1993, the book business had so outgrown its shelf that Martinez decided to put down his shears and turn the shop into a bookstore. He began hosting readings and community events, and Libreria Martinez was soon thronged with people. Martinez was fast becoming a leading advocate of literacy and cultural education in the Latino community. From 1997 until 2001, he partnered with actor Edward James Olmos to establish the Latino Book and Family Festival. It has since become the country's largest Spanish-language book

exposition, now held regularly in four states. (You've got to love a guy who teams up with Lt. Martin Castillo of *Miami Vice*.)

Martinez, who left the festival to focus on his business, has three stores in California now, including one that focuses on children's books. Combined, they generate nearly $1 million in annual sales. He would like to have as many as 25 locations by 2012. "The plan is that if a new store meets its goals, we'll open another," he says. And though business is booming, Martinez, who is now 65, still likes to make time to cut hair for some of his longtime customers. "If I cut one or two haircuts a month, I'm in heaven," he says. Of course, while he trims away, he also recommends a couple of good reads.

"Most Fascinating Entrepreneurs" by Jeffrey L. Seglin from *Inc* Magazine, April 2005. Reprinted by permission of *Inc* Magazine via Copyright Clearance Center.

Jesuit Greg Boyle, Gang Priest

A movie's in the offing, but the work done by this Jesuit priest is far from the glamour of Hollywood. His ministry with gangs is a daily walk to the edge—a walk of love.

By Carol Ann Morrow

It helps to have connections if you want to meet the Rev. Greg Boyle, S.J.—gang connections. Father Greg doesn't have much time to tell his story to *St. Anthony Messenger*. Why? Because he gives—and gives and gives—his time, his energy and his influence (known in the neighborhood as "juice") to the young people of the Pico/Aliso District in East L.A.

Pico Gardens and Aliso Village, sometimes called "The Projects," is the largest tract of subsidized housing west of the Mississippi. This huge piece of social engineering hasn't worked out so well. It's poor, crowded and packed with gangs.

Some of Pico/Aliso overlaps Boyle Heights (different era, different Boyle). Within those 16 square miles, 60 gangs claim 10,000 members, Hispanic and black. This equals violence and plenty of action at the Hollenbeck division of the Los Angeles Police Department—if Father Greg Boyle doesn't get there first.

In two days hanging around Father Greg's office, a modest though vividly painted storefront on L.A.'s East First Street, G-Dog or G, as the kids affectionately call the Jesuit, reveals life in a very fast lane. The priest's office—nine feet square maximum—is a windowless, unfinished drywall box in the epicenter of the 600-square-foot headquarters of Jobs for a Future (JFF). He has an open door in—and an open door beyond—to other offices, storage for Homeboy Industries silkscreened items and the only bathroom. Traffic through Greg's doorway feels as hectic as the L.A. freeway system.

Father Greg requests, "Hold my calls." But when a prison inmate gets a chance to phone, the priest reneges, "Well, let me take just this one. . . ." A young man comes by—dressed for success—to tell his happy story and thank Father Greg for the contact, the clothes, a job, a hope. With Greg on the phone and me in the visitor's chair, the young man preens back and forth between the front and back doors of this short runway. He and the priest exchange a complex handshake, a triumphant smile, a thumbs-up. No words seem necessary. Pride is evident in both son—and father. Father Greg is surrogate parent to hundreds of Hispanic youth, many the children of Latino immigrants.

The office is crammed with memorabilia which I study while he's on the phone. Official framed certificates, plaques and news clippings hang next to drawings by—and photos of—neighborhood youth. Latin American artifacts and activist posters jockey for wall space with strong, distinctive samples of graffiti wall art. The colorful sketches Father Greg has pinned to the wall have no ominous overtones, however. His poorly lit office is bright with evidence of love.

How can Father Greg take time to talk about what's already happened when more is happening—right now? How can he speak of his dreams when young dreamers are lined up outside the door? "So—what do you want to know?" he asks as he hangs up the phone, signs some kind of permission slip for a girl's school function, hollers out with pseudo-sternness, "No more calls!" and tries to fit the story of his life into the 10 minutes before he dashes to another appointment.

Directions:

1. Read each paragraph.

2. After reading a paragraph, write an adjective that best describes Lincoln as he is described in that paragraph.

3. Before moving on to the next paragraph, underline words in the paragraph that relate to that adjective you jotted down in Step 2.

4. When you finish the article, circle the most important adjectives.

5. Write a paragraph that explains how those qualities (the adjectives you chose) contribute to success. Be sure your paragraph has a focus, or main idea. Provide examples and discuss how each example relates to the main idea.

LEADERS AND SUCCESS: Abraham Lincoln

By Michael Mink

When faced with disadvantages, some people complain.

And then there was Abraham Lincoln. Complaining didn't occur to him—not when he could take the same disadvantages and make them opportunities.

The biggest obstacle Lincoln (1809-65) had to overcome was his own humble beginnings. Born into poverty, to illiterate parents, his formal schooling totaled less than a year. But he had a powerful ambition to achieve, and a yearning to make the world a better place.

The answer for Lincoln was literally all there in black and white, in the form of the books he learned to cherish. As a boy, he resolved to educate himself. As a man, he never stopped adding to his store of knowledge.

"The mode is very simple, though laborious and tedious. It is only to get the books, and read, and study them carefully. . . Work, work, work, is the main thing," Lincoln said. "A capacity, and taste, for reading gives access to whatever has already been discovered by others. It is the key, or one of the keys, to the already solved problems. And not only so. It gives a relish, and facility, for successfully pursuing the unsolved ones."

Preparing for Life

Lincoln focused on books that helped prepare him for the life he wanted to lead, that of a public man serving society. "Lincoln preferred breadth to depth . . . targeted reading . . . and realized that the world's greatest achievers were totally immersed in their respective subjects," wrote Gene Griessman in *The Words Lincoln Lived By.*

Lincoln undertook the study of law on his own because he felt the profession offered him a chance to contribute to the greater good. "For Lincoln, his vocation became a way to make a difference," Griessman wrote.

The discipline required to educate himself gave Lincoln the foundation to succeed. He built on his education with ambition. "Do you suppose that I should ever have got (noticed) if I had waited to be hunted up and pushed forward by older men?" he said.

Lincoln wasn't afraid to take unpopular political positions if he deemed them correct, and his nickname of "Honest Abe" wasn't rooted in myth or political propaganda, but in reality.

"I have always wanted to deal with everyone I meet candidly and honestly. If I have made any assertion not warranted by facts, and it is pointed out to me, I will withdraw it cheerfully," Lincoln said. "Resolve to be honest at all events: if, in your own judgment, you cannot be an honest lawyer, resolve to be honest without being a lawyer."

"Lincoln cultivated the reputation of being an honest man. People trusted him," said Phillip Shaw Paludan, a Lincoln and Civil War scholar and author of *The Presidency of Abraham Lincoln.*

As a result, history reveres him. As the 16th U.S. president (1861-65), it was Lincoln who remained steadfast when it came to holding the union together. His Emancipation Proclamation helped bring 4 million slaves to freedom and end slavery. His kindness, intelligence and self-deprecating humor have left a treasure of speeches and letters that have been the basis for

LEADERS AND SUCCESS: Abraham Lincoln (page 2)

thousands of books about him (only Jesus and Shakespeare have had more). He's perhaps the greatest presidential writer. Most historians rank Lincoln among the greatest, if not the greatest, of the presidents.

"There's a certain tenacity in the man that is just overwhelming," Paludan said.

Upon his election to the presidency in 1860, and with the onset of the Civil War, Lincoln was the object of Southern scorn and ridicule. He was even subjected to jeers in the North, and sometimes by his own Cabinet members and generals. While the attacks against him personally could be harsh and cruel, Lincoln ignored them.

"He very seldom took anything personally in politics. Lincoln said he believed in short statutes of limitations in politics, meaning if somebody attacked him, he knew the political context for it and he just didn't take it personally," Paludan said. "That allowed him to not answer vitriol with vitriol, but to get along with people, and to get along with people he had to get along with, rather than making enemies in Congress or any other place."

Throughout the war, Lincoln spoke only of charity and good will toward the South. "I shall do nothing in malice. What I deal with is too vast for malicious dealing," Lincoln said in 1862.

Bridge Building

After Lee's surrender at Appomattox, and literally hours before he was assassinated, Lincoln refused to condone retaliation against the leaders of the Confederacy.

"I hope there will be no persecution, no bloody work after the war is over. None need expect me to take part in hanging or killing them. Enough lives have been sacrificed. We must extinguish our resentment if we expect harmony and union," Lincoln told his Cabinet.

Even as he became a world figure, Lincoln maintained his modesty. He discouraged the many titles conferred on him in private, such as "The Honorable," or "Mr. President." He enjoyed meeting everyday people and treated them with the same respect and care as he did political and military leaders. "Men moving only in an official circle are apt to become merely official . . . (and) forget that they only hold power in a representative capacity," Lincoln said.

"In my life I have seen a good number of men distinguished by their talents or their station," wrote London journalist Edward Dicey, as quoted by Griessman. "But I never saw any one, so apparently unconscious that this distinction conferred upon him any superiority, as Abraham Lincoln."

Lincoln was secure enough to admit what he didn't know. For example, he asked his secretary of state and one-time political rival, William Seward, to tutor him in areas of government and politics he felt he needed help in. Seward, a college graduate, was a former New York governor and U.S. senator. Lincoln drilled him with questions.

"(Lincoln) brought to every question the same patient inquiry into details, the same eager longing to know and do exactly what was just and right, and the same working-day, plodding, laborious devotion, which characterized his management of a client's case in Springfield," wrote then-New York Times editor Henry J. Raymond.

In the end, Lincoln achieved the goal in life he set out for himself: "I have an irrepressible desire to live until I can be assured that the world is a little better for my having lived in it," he said.

(*Investor's Business Daily*, February 13, 2005)

We live in an age of unprecedented opportunity: If you've got ambition and smarts, you can rise to the top of your chosen profession, regardless of where you started out.

But with opportunity comes responsibility. Companies today aren't managing their employees' careers; knowledge workers must, effectively, be their own chief executive officers. It's up to you to carve out your place, to know when to change course, and to keep yourself engaged and productive during a work life that may span some 50 years. To do those things well, you'll need to cultivate a deep understanding of yourself—not only what your strengths and weaknesses are but also how you learn, how you work with others, what your values are, and where you can make the greatest contribution. Because only when you operate from strengths can you achieve true excellence.

Managing Oneself

by Peter F. Drucker

Success in the knowledge economy comes to those who know themselves—their strengths, their values, and how they best perform.

History's great achievers—a Napoleon, a da Vinci, a Mozart—have always managed themselves. That, in large measure, is what makes them great achievers. But they are rare exceptions, so unusual both in their talents and their accomplishments as to be considered outside the boundaries of ordinary human existence. Now, most of us, even those of us with modest endowments, will have to learn to manage ourselves. We will have to learn to develop ourselves. We will have to place ourselves where we can make the greatest contribution. And we will have to stay mentally alert and engaged during a 50-year working life, which means knowing how and when to change the work we do.

What Are My Strengths?

Most people think they know what they are good at. They are usually wrong. More often, people know what they are not good at—and even then more people are wrong than right. And yet, a person can perform only from strength. One cannot build performance on weaknesses, let alone on something one cannot do at all.

Throughout history, people had little need to know their strengths. A person was born into a position and a line of work: The peasant's son would also be a peasant; the artisan's daughter, an artisan's wife; and so on. But now people have choices. We need to know our strengths in order to know where we belong.

The only way to discover your strengths is through feedback analysis. Whenever you make a key decision or take a key action, write

Reprinted by permission of *Harvard Business Review*. From "Managing Oneself" by Peter F. Drucker, January, 2005. © 2005 by the Harvard Business School Publishing Corporation; all rights reserved.

down what you expect will happen. Nine or 12 months later, compare the actual results with your expectations. I have been practicing this method for 15 to 20 years now, and every time I do it, I am surprised. The feedback analysis showed me, for instance—and to my great surprise—that I have an intuitive understanding of technical people, whether they are engineers or accountants or market researchers. It also showed me that I don't really resonate with generalists.

Feedback analysis is by no means new. It was invented sometime in the fourteenth century by an otherwise totally obscure German theologian and picked up quite independently, some 150 years later, by John Calvin and Ignatius of Loyola, each of whom incorporated it into the practice of his followers. In fact, the steadfast focus on performance and results that this habit produces explains why the institutions these two men founded, the Calvinist church and the Jesuit order, came to dominate Europe within 30 years.

Practiced consistently, this simple method will show you within a fairly short period of time, maybe two or three years, where your strengths lie—and this is the most important thing to know. The method will show you what you are doing or failing to do that deprives you of the full benefits of your strengths. It will show you where you are not particularly competent. And finally, it will show you where you have no strengths and cannot perform.

Several implications for action follow from feedback analysis. First and foremost, concentrate on your strengths. Put yourself where your strengths can produce results.

Second, work on improving your strengths. Analysis will rapidly show where you need to improve skills or acquire new ones. It will also show the gaps in your knowledge—and those can usually be filled. Mathematicians are born, but everyone can learn trigonometry.

Third, discover where your intellectual arrogance is causing disabling ignorance and overcome it. Far too many people—especially people with great expertise in one area—are contemptuous of knowledge in other areas or believe that being bright is a substitute for knowledge. First-rate engineers, for instance, tend to take pride in not knowing anything about people. Human beings, they believe, are much too disorderly for the good engineering mind. Human resources professionals, by contrast, often pride themselves on their ignorance of elementary accounting or of quantitative methods altogether. But taking pride in such ignorance is self-defeating. Go to work on acquiring the skills and knowledge you need to fully realize your strengths.

It is equally essential to remedy your bad habits—the things you do or fail to do that inhibit your effectiveness and performance. Such habits will quickly show up in the feedback. For example, a planner may find that his beautiful plans fail because he does not follow through on them. Like so many brilliant people, he believes that ideas move mountains. But bulldozers move mountains; ideas show where the bulldozers should go to work. This planner will have to learn that the work does not stop when the plan is completed. He must find people to carry out the plan and explain it to them. He must adapt and change it as he puts it into action. And finally, he must decide when to stop pushing the plan.

At the same time, feedback will also reveal when the problem is a lack of manners. Manners are the lubricating oil of an organization. It is a law of nature that two moving bodies in contact with each other create friction. This is as true for human beings as it is for inanimate objects. Manners—simple things like saying "please" and "thank you" and knowing a person's name or asking after her family—enable two people to work together whether they like each other or not. Bright people, especially bright young people, often do not understand this. If analysis shows that someone's brilliant work fails again and again as soon as cooperation from others is required, it probably indicates a lack of courtesy—that is, a lack of manners.

Comparing your expectations with your results also indicates what not to do. We all have a vast number of areas in which we have no talent or skill and little chance of becoming even mediocre. In those areas a person—and especially a knowledge worker—should not take on work, jobs, and assignments. One should waste as little effort as possible on improving areas of low competence. It takes far more energy and work to improve from incompetence to mediocrity than it takes to improve from first-rate performance to

Managing Oneself (page 3)

excellence. And yet most people—especially most teachers and most organizations—concentrate on making incompetent performers into mediocre ones. Energy, resources, and time should go instead to making a competent person into a star performer.

How Do I Perform?

Amazingly few people know how they get things done. Indeed, most of us do not even know that different people work and perform differently. Too many people work in ways that are not their ways, and that almost guarantees nonperformance. For knowledge workers, How do I perform? may be an even more important question than What are my strengths?

Like one's strengths, how one performs is unique. It is a matter of personality. Whether personality be a matter of nature or nurture, it surely is formed long before a person goes to work. And how a person performs is a given, just as what a person is good at or not good at is a given. A person's way of performing can be slightly modified, but it is unlikely to be completely changed—and certainly not easily. Just as people achieve results by doing what they are good at, they also achieve results by working in ways that they best perform. A few common personality traits usually determine how a person performs.

Am I a reader or a listener? The first thing to know is whether you are a reader or a listener. Far too few people even know that there are readers and listeners and that people are rarely both. Even fewer know which of the two they themselves are. But some examples will show how damaging such ignorance can be.

When Dwight Eisenhower was Supreme Commander of the Allied forces in Europe, he was the darling of the press. His press conferences were famous for their style—General Eisenhower showed total command of whatever question he was asked, and he was able to describe a situation and explain a policy in two or three beautifully polished and elegant sentences. Ten years later, the same journalists who had been his admirers held President Eisenhower in open contempt. He never addressed the questions, they complained, but rambled on endlessly about something else. And they constantly ridiculed him for butchering the King's English in incoherent and ungrammatical answers.

Eisenhower apparently did not know that he was a reader, not a listener. When he was Supreme Commander in Europe, his aides made sure that every question from the press was presented in writing at least half an hour before a conference was to begin. And then Eisenhower was in total command. When he became president, he succeeded two listeners, Franklin D. Roosevelt and Harry Truman. Both men knew themselves to be listeners and both enjoyed free-for-all press conferences. Eisenhower may have felt that he had to do what his two predecessors had done. As a result, he never even heard the questions journalists asked. And Eisenhower is not even an extreme case of a nonlistener.

A few years later, Lyndon Johnson destroyed his presidency, in large measure, by not knowing that he was a listener. His predecessor, John Kennedy, was a reader who had assembled a brilliant group of writers as his assistants, making sure that they wrote to him before discussing their memos in person. Johnson kept these people on his staff—and they kept on writing. He never, apparently, understood one word of what they wrote. Yet as a senator, Johnson had been superb; for parliamentarians have to be, above all, listeners.

Few listeners can be made, or can make themselves, into competent readers—and vice versa. The listener who tries to be a reader will,

Do not try to change yourself—you are unlikely to succeed. Work to improve the way you perform.

therefore, suffer the fate of Lyndon Johnson, whereas the reader who tries to be a listener will suffer the fate of Dwight Eisenhower. They will not perform or achieve.

How do I learn?

The second thing to know about how one performs is to know how one learns. Many first-class writers—Winston Churchill is but one example—do poorly in school. They tend to remember their schooling as pure torture. Yet few of their classmates remember it the same way. They may not have enjoyed the school very much, but the worst they suffered was boredom. The explanation is that writers do not, as a rule, learn by listening and reading. They learn by writing. Because schools do not allow them to learn this way, they get poor grades.

Schools everywhere are organized on the assumption that there is only one right way to learn and that it is the same way for everybody. But to be forced to learn the way a school teaches is sheer hell for students who learn differently. Indeed, there are probably half a dozen different ways to learn.

There are people, like Churchill, who learn by writing. Some people learn by taking copious notes. Beethoven, for example, left behind an enormous number of sketchbooks, yet he said he never actually looked at them when he composed. Asked why he kept them, he is reported to have replied, "If I don't write it down immediately, I forget it right away. If I put it into a sketchbook, I never forget it and I never have to look it up again." Some people learn by doing. Others learn by hearing themselves talk.

A chief executive I know who converted a small and mediocre family business into the leading company in its industry was one of those people who learn by talking. He was in the habit of calling his entire senior staff into his office once a week and then talking at them for two or three hours. He would raise policy issues and argue three different positions on each one. He rarely asked his associates for comments or questions; he sim-

ply needed an audience to hear himself talk. That's how he learned. And although he is a fairly extreme case, learning through talking is by no means an unusual method. Successful trial lawyers learn the same way, as do many medical diagnosticians (and so do I).

Of all the important pieces of self-knowledge, understanding how you learn is the easiest to acquire. When I ask people, "How do you learn?" most of them know the answer. But when I ask, "Do you act on this knowledge?" few answer yes. And yet, acting on this knowledge is the key to performance; or rather, *not* acting on this knowledge condemns one to nonperformance.

Am I a reader or a listener? and How do I learn? are the first questions to ask. But they are by no means the only ones. To manage yourself effectively, you also have to ask, Do I work well with people, or am I a loner? And if you do work well with people, you then must ask, In what relationship?

Some people work best as subordinates. General George Patton, the great American military hero of World War II, is a prime example. Patton was America's top troop commander. Yet when he was proposed for an independent command, General George Marshall, the U.S. chief of staff—and probably the most successful picker of men in U.S. history—said, "Patton is the best subordinate the American army has ever produced, but he would be the worst commander."

Some people work best as team members. Others work best alone. Some are exceptionally talented as

coaches and mentors; others are simply incompetent as mentors.

Another crucial question is, Do I produce results as a decision maker or as an adviser? A great many people perform best as advisers but cannot take the burden and pressure of making the decision. A good many other people, by contrast, need an adviser to force themselves to think; then they can make decisions and act on them with speed, self-confidence, and courage.

This is a reason, by the way, that the number two person in an organization often fails when promoted to the number one position. The top spot requires a decision maker. Strong decision makers often put somebody they trust into the number two spot as their adviser —and in that position the person is outstanding. But in the number one spot, the same person fails. He or she knows what the decision should be but cannot accept the responsibility of actually making it.

Other important questions to ask include, Do I perform well under stress, or do I need a highly structured and predictable environment? Do I work best in a big organization or a small one? Few people work well in all kinds of environments. Again and again, I have seen people who were very successful in large organizations flounder miserably when they moved into smaller ones. And the reverse is equally true.

The conclusion bears repeating: Do not try to change yourself—you are unlikely to succeed. But work hard to improve the way you perform. And try not to take on work you cannot perform or will only perform poorly.

What Are My Values?

To be able to manage yourself, you finally have to ask, What are my values? This is not a question of ethics. With respect to ethics, the rules are the same for everybody, and the test is a simple one. I call it the "mirror test."

In the early years of this century, the most highly respected diplomat of all the great powers was the German ambassador in London. He was clearly destined for great things—to become his country's foreign minister, at least, if not its federal chancellor. Yet in 1906 he abruptly resigned rather than preside over a dinner given by the diplomatic corps for Edward VII. The king was a notorious womanizer and made it clear what kind of dinner he wanted. The ambassador is reported to have said, "I refuse to see a pimp in the mirror in the morning when I shave."

That is the mirror test. Ethics requires that you ask yourself, What kind of person do I want to see in the mirror in the morning? What is ethical behavior in one kind of organization or situation is ethical behavior in another. But ethics is only part of a value system—especially of an organization's value system.

To work in an organization whose value system is unacceptable or incompatible with one's own condemns a person both to frustration and to nonperformance.

Consider the experience of a highly successful human resources executive whose company was acquired by a bigger organization.

After the acquisition, she was promoted to do the kind of work she did best, which included selecting people for important positions. The executive deeply believed that a company should hire people for such positions from the outside only after exhausting all the inside possibilities. But her new company believed in first looking outside "to bring in fresh blood." There is something to be said for both approaches—in my experience, the proper one is to do some of both. They are, however, fundamentally incompatible—not as policies but as values. They bespeak different views of the relationship between organizations and people; different views of the responsibility of an

What one does well— even very well and successfully—may not fit with one's value system.

organization to its people and their development; and different views of a person's most important contribution to an enterprise. After several years of frustration, the executive quit—at considerable financial loss. Her values and the values of the organization simply were not compatible.

Similarly, whether a pharmaceutical company tries to obtain results by making constant, small improvements or by achieving occasional, highly expensive, and risky "breakthroughs" is not primarily an economic question. The results of either strategy may be pretty much the same. At bottom,

there is a conflict between a value system that sees the company's contribution in terms of helping physicians do better what they already do and a value system that is oriented toward making scientific discoveries.

Whether a business should be run for short-term results or with a focus on the long term is likewise a question of values. Financial analysts believe that businesses can be run for both simultaneously. Successful businesspeople know better. To be sure, every company has to produce short-term results. But in any conflict between short-term results and long-term growth, each company will determine its own priority. This is not primarily a disagreement about economics. It is fundamentally a value conflict regarding the function of a business and the responsibility of management.

Value conflicts are not limited to business organizations. One of the fastest-growing pastoral churches in the United States measures success by the number of new parishioners. Its leadership believes that what matters is how many newcomers join the congregation. The Good Lord will then minister to their spiritual needs or at least to the needs of a sufficient percentage. Another pastoral, evangelical church believes that what matters is people's spiritual growth. The church eases out newcomers who join but do not enter into its spiritual life.

Again, this is not a matter of numbers. At first glance, it appears that the second church grows more slowly. But it retains a far larger proportion of newcomers than the first one does. Its growth, in other words, is more solid. This is also not a theological problem, or only secondarily so. It is a problem about values. In a public debate, one pastor argued, "Unless you first come to church, you will never find the gate to the Kingdom of Heaven."

"No," answered the other. "Until you first look for the gate to the Kingdom of Heaven, you don't belong in church."

Organizations, like people, have values. To be effective in an organization, a person's values must be compatible with the organization's values. They do not need to be the same, but they must be close enough to coexist. Otherwise, the person will not only be frustrated but also will not produce results.

A person's strengths and the way that person performs rarely conflict; the two are complementary. But there is sometimes a conflict between a person's values and his or her strengths. What one does well—even very well and successfully—may not fit with one's value system. In that case, the work may not appear to be worth devoting one's life to (or even a substantial portion thereof).

If I may, allow me to interject a personal note. Many years ago, I too had to decide between my values and what I was doing successfully. I was doing very well as a young investment banker in London in the mid-1930s, and the work clearly fit my strengths. Yet I did not see myself making a contribution as an asset manager. People, I realized, were what I valued, and I saw no point in being the richest man in the cemetery. I had no

money and no other job prospects. Despite the continuing Depression, I quit—and it was the right thing to do. Values, in other words, are and should be the ultimate test.

Where Do I Belong?

A small number of people know very early where they belong. Mathematicians, musicians, and cooks, for instance, are usually mathematicians, musicians, and cooks by the time they are four or five years old. Physicians usually decide on their careers in their teens, if not earlier. But most people, especially highly gifted people, do not really know where they belong until they are well past their mid-twenties. By that time, however, they should know the answers to the three questions: What are my strengths? How do I perform? and, What are my values? And then they can and should decide where they belong.

Or rather, they should be able to decide where they do *not* belong. The person who has learned that he or she does not perform well in a big organization should have learned to say no to a position in one. The person who has learned that he or she is not a decision maker should have learned to say no to a decision-making assignment. A General Patton (who probably never learned this himself) should have learned to say no to an independent command.

Equally important, knowing the answer to these questions enables a person to say to an opportunity, an offer, or an assignment, "Yes, I will do that. But this is the way I should be doing it. This is the way it should

be structured. This is the way the relationships should be. These are the kindS of results you should expect from me, and in this time frame, because this is who I am."

Successful careers are not planned. They develop when people are prepared for opportunities because they know their strengths, their method of work, and their values. Knowing,where one belongs can transform an ordinary person—hardworking and competent but otherwise mediocre—into an outstanding performer.

What Should I Contribute?

Throughout history, the great majority of people never had to ask the question, What should I contribute? They were told what to contribute, and their tasks were dictated either by the work itself—as it was for the peasant or artisan—or by a master or a mistress—as it was for domestic servants. And until very recently, it was taken for granted that most people were subordinates who did as they were told. Even in the 1950s and 1960s, the new knowledge workers (the so-called organization men) looked to their company's personnel department to plan their careers.

Then in the late 1960s, no one wanted to be told what to do any longer. Young men and women began to ask, What do I want to do? And what they heard was that the way to contribute was to "do your own thing." But this solution was as wrong as the organization men's had been. Very few of the people who believed that doing one's own thing would lead to contribution, self-fulfillment, and success achieved any of the three.

But still, there is no return to the old answer of doing what you are told or assigned to do. Knowledge workers in particular have to learn to ask a question that has not been asked before: What *should* my contribution be? To answer it, they must address three distinct elements: What does the situation require? Given my strengths, my way of performing, and my values, how can I make the greatest contribution to what needs to be done? And finally, What results have to be achieved to make a difference?

Consider the experience of a newly appointed hospital administrator. The hospital was big and prestigious, but it had been coasting on its reputation for 30 years. The new administrator decided that his contribution should be to establish a standard of excellence in one important area within two years. He chose to focus on the emergency room, which was big, visible, and sloppy. He decided that every patient who came into the ER had to be seen by a qualified nurse within 60 seconds. Within 12 months, the hospital's emergency room had become a model for all hospitals in the United States, and within another two years, the whole hospital had been transformed.

As this example suggests, it is rarely possible—or even particularly fruitful—to look too far ahead. A plan can usually cover no more than 18 months and still be reasonably clear and specific. So the question in most cases should be, Where and how can I achieve results that will make a difference within the next year and a half? The answer must balance several things. First, the results should be hard to achieve—they should require "stretching," to use the current buzzword. But also, they should be within reach. To aim at results that cannot be achieved—or that can be only under the most unlikely circumstances—is not being ambitious; it is being foolish. Second, the results should be meaningful. They should make a difference. Finally, results should be visible and, if at all possible, measurable. From this will come a course of action: what to do, where and how to start, and what goals and deadlines to set.

Responsibility for Relationships

Very few people work by themselves and achieve results by themselves—a few great artists, a few great scientists, a few great athletes. Most people work with others and are effective with other people. That is true whether they are members of an organization or independently employed. Managing yourself requires taking responsibility for relationships. This has two parts.

The first is to accept the fact that other people are as much individuals as you yourself are. They perversely insist on behaving like human beings. This means that they too have their strengths; they too have their ways of getting things done; they too have their values. To be effective, therefore, you have to know the strengths, the performance modes, and the values of your coworkers.

That sounds obvious, but few people pay attention to it. Typical is the person who was trained to write reports in his or her first assignment because that boss was a reader. Even if the next boss is a listener, the person goes on writing reports that, invariably, produce no results. Invariably the boss will think the employee is stupid, incompetent, and lazy, and he or she will fail. But that could have been avoided if the employee had only looked at the new boss and analyzed how *this* boss performs.

Bosses are neither a title on the organization chart nor a "function." They are individuals and are entitled to do their work in the way they do it best. It is incumbent on the people who work with them to observe them, to find out how they work, and to adapt themselves to what makes their bosses most effective. This, in fact, is the secret of "managing" the boss.

The same holds true for all your coworkers. Each works his or her way, not your way. And each is entitled to work in his or her way. What matters is whether they perform and what their values are. As for how they perform—each is likely to do it differently. The first secret of effectiveness is to understand the people you work with and depend on so that you can make use of their strengths, their ways of working, and their values. Working relationships are as much based on the people as they are on the work.

The second part of relationship responsibility is taking responsibility for communication. Whenever I, or any other consultant, start to work with an organization, the first thing I hear about are all the personality conflicts. Most of these arise from the fact that people do not know what other people are doing and how they do their work, or what contribution the other people are concentrating on and what

The first secret of effectiveness is to understand the people you work with so that you can make use of their strengths.

results they expect. And the reason they do not know is that they have not asked and therefore have not been told.

This failure to ask reflects human stupidity less than it reflects human history. Until recently, it was unnecessary to tell any of these things to anybody. In the medieval city, everyone in a district plied the same trade. In the countryside, everyone in a valley planted the same crop as soon as the frost was out of the ground. Even those few people who did things that were not "common" worked alone, so they did not have to tell anyone what they were doing.

Today the great majority of people work with others who have different tasks and responsibilities. The marketing vice president may have come out of sales and know everything about sales, but she knows nothing about the things she has never done—pricing, advertising, packaging, and the like. So the people who do these things must make sure that the marketing vice president understands what they

are trying to do, why they are trying to do it, how they are going to do it, and what results to expect.

If the marketing vice president does not understand what these high-grade knowledge specialists are doing, it is primarily their fault, not hers. They have not educated her. Conversely, it is the marketing vice president's responsibility to make sure that all of her coworkers understand how she looks at marketing: what her goals are, how she works, and what she expects of herself and of each one of them.

Even people who understand the importance of taking responsibility for relationships often do not communicate sufficiently with their associates. They are afraid of being thought presumptuous or inquisitive or stupid. They are wrong. Whenever someone goes to his or her associates and says, "This is what I am good at. This is how I work. These are my values. This is the contribution I plan to concentrate on and the results I should be expected to deliver," the response is always, "This is most helpful. But why didn't you tell me earlier?"

And one gets the same reaction—without exception, in my experience—if one continues by asking, "And what do I need to know about your strengths, how you perform, your values, and your proposed contribution?" In fact, knowledge

workers should request this of everyone with whom they work, whether as subordinate, superior, colleague, or team member. And again, whenever this is done, the reaction is always, "Thanks for asking me. But why didn't you ask me earlier?"

Organizations are no longer built on force but on trust. The existence of trust between people does not necessarily mean that they like one another. It means that they understand one another. Taking responsibility for relationships is therefore an absolute necessity. It is a duty. Whether one is a member of the organization, a consultant to it, a supplier, or a distributor, one owes that responsibility to all one's coworkers: those whose work one depends on as well as those who depend on one's own work.

The Second Half of Your Life

When work for most people meant manual labor, there was no need to worry about the second half of your life. You simply kept on doing what you had always done. And if you were lucky enough to survive 40 years of hard work in the mill or on the railroad, you were quite happy to spend the rest of your life doing nothing. Today, however, most work is knowledge work, and knowledge workers are not "finished" after 40 years on the job, they are merely bored.

We hear a great deal of talk about the midlife crisis of the executive. It is mostly boredom. At 45, most executives have reached the peak of their business careers, and they know it. After 20 years of doing very much the same kind of work, they are very good at their jobs. But they are not learning or contributing or deriving challenge and satisfaction from the job. And yet they are still likely to face another 20 if not 25 years of work. That is why managing oneself increasingly leads one to begin a second career.

There are three ways to develop a second career. The first is actually to start one. Often this takes nothing more than moving from one kind of organization to another. the

a parallel career. Many people who are very successful in their first careers stay in the work they have been doing, either on a full-time or part-time or consulting basis. But in addition, they create a parallel job, usually in a nonprofit organization, that takes another ten hours of work a week. They might take over the administration of their church, for instance, or the presidency of the local Girl Scouts council. They might run the battered women's shelter, work as a children's librari-

minority. The majority may "retire on the job" and count the years until their actual retirement. But it is this minority, the men and women who see a long working-life expectancy as an opportunity both for themselves and for society, who will become leaders and models.

There is one prerequisite for managing the second half of your life: You must begin long before you enter it. When it first became clear 30 years ago that working-life expectancies were lengthening very fast, many observers (including myself) believed that retired people would increasingly become volunteers for nonprofit institutions. That has not happened. If one does not begin to volunteer before one is 40 or so, one will not volunteer once past 60.

There is one prerequisite for managing the second half of your life: You must begin doing so long before you enter it.

divisional controller in a large corporation, for instance, becomes the controller of a medium-sized hospital. But there are also growing numbers of people who move into different lines of work altogether: the business executive or government official who enters the ministry at 45, for instance, or the midlevel manager who leaves corporate life after 20 years to attend law school and become a small-town attorney.

We will see many more second careers undertaken by people who have achieved modest success in their first jobs. Such people have substantial skills, and they know how to work. They need a community—the house is empty with the children gone—and they need income as well. But above all, they need challenge.

The second way to prepare for the second half of your life is to develop

an for the local public library, sit on the school board, and so on.

Finally, there are the social entrepreneurs. These are usually people who have been very successful in their first careers. They love their work, but it no longer challenges them. In many cases they keep on doing what they have been doing all along but spend less and less of their time on it. They also start another activity, usually a nonprofit. My friend Bob Buford, for example, built a very successful television company that he still runs. But he has also founded and built a successful nonprofit organization that works with Protestant churches, and he is building another to teach social entrepreneurs how to manage their own nonprofit ventures while still running their original businesses.

People who manage the second half of their lives may always be a

Similarly, all the social entrepreneurs I know began to work in their chosen second enterprise long before they reached their peak in their original business. Consider the example of a successful lawyer, the legal counsel to a large corporation, who has started a venture to establish model schools in his state. He began to do volunteer legal work for the schools when he was around 35. He was elected to the school board at age 40. At age 50, when he had amassed a fortune, he started his own enterprise to build and to run model schools. He is, however, still working nearly full-time as the lead counsel in the company he helped found as a young lawyer.

There is another reason to develop a second major interest, and to develop it early. No one can expect to live very long without experiencing a serious setback in his or her life or work. There is the competent engineer who is passed over for promotion at age 45. There is the competent college professor who realizes at age 42 that she will never get a professorship at a big university, even though she may be fully qualified for it. There are tragedies in one's family life: the breakup of one's marriage or the loss of a child. At such times, a second major interest—not just a hobby—may make all the difference. The engineer, for example, now knows that he has not been very successful in his job. But in his outside activity—as church treasurer, for example—he is a success. One's family may break up, but in that outside activity there is still a community. In a society in which success has become so terribly important, having options will become increasingly vital. Historically, there was no such thing as "success." The overwhelming majority of people did not expect anything but to stay in their "proper station," as an old English prayer has it. The only mobility was downward mobility.

In a knowledge society, however, we expect everyone to be a success. This is clearly an impossibility. For a great many people, there is at best an absence of failure. Wherever there is success, there has to be failure. And then it is vitally important for the individual, and equally for the individual's family, to have an area in which he or she can contribute, make a difference, and be *somebody*. That means finding a second area—whether in a second career, a parallel career, or a social venture—that offers an opportunity for being a leader, for being respected, for being a success.

The challenges of managing oneself may seem obvious, if not elementary. And the answers may seem self-evident to the point of appearing naive. But managing oneself requires new and unprecedented things from the individual, and especially from the knowledge worker. In effect, managing oneself demands that each knowledge worker think and behave like a chief executive officer. Further, the shift from manual workers who do as they are told to knowledge workers who have to manage themselves profoundly challenges social structure. Every existing society, even the most individualistic one, takes two things for granted, if only subconsciously: that organizations outlive workers, and that most people stay put.But today the opposite is true. Knowledge workers outlive organizations, and they are mobile. The need to manage oneself is therefore creating a revolution in human affairs.

Peter F. Drucker is the Marie Rankin Clarke Professor of Social Science and Management (Emeritus) at Claremont Graduate University in Claremont, California. This article is an excerpt from his book Management Challenges for the 21st Century *(HarperCollins, 1999).*

MEASURE OF A MAN'S LIFE

Questions of redemption, atonement and clemency swirl as
Stanley Tookie Williams' execution date approaches

AS A CRIMINAL

By Leslie Fulbright, Chronicle Staff Writer

For more than 20 years, Rebecca Owens thought the man who murdered her father had been executed.

She was 8 when her dad was shot twice in the back with a shotgun during a 4 a.m. robbery at a 7-Eleven store near Los Angeles.

"I grew up being told the killer was dead," Owens, now 35, said in a recent telephone interview. "They told me he was killed right after my father."

Owens didn't learn that Stanley Tookie Williams, the man convicted of the murder, was still alive until she got a call from the state attorney general's office about four years ago. Not only was he alive, she was told, but he was about to be featured on a news program for his Nobel Peace Prize nomination.

"I lost it," Owens said. "I didn't know he was alive, much less nominated for a peace prize. I searched his name on Google and I found out they were making a movie about him too, about his redemption."

Williams, the admitted co-founder of the Crips gang, was convicted of killing Owens' father and three members of another family in a second robbery 26 years ago. He has pleaded with Gov. Arnold Schwarzenegger to spare him from his scheduled Dec. 13 execution, saying his efforts to keep young people from following him into gang life merit mercy.

Owens doesn't buy it.

"He killed my father, and that will never change," she said. "I think he is a horrible and awful man.

"I don't think it's fair that he gets to breathe and walk around and have interactions, and my father, whose only crime was showing up for work, can't do those things," Owens said. "The impact that my father's death had on me is long-reaching and affects me today."

Albert Lewis Owens was 26 years old and working the graveyard shift early Feb. 27, 1979, sweeping the parking lot at a 7-Eleven on Whittier Boulevard, when two men entered the store. He put down the broom and followed them inside.

The men were approaching the cash register when a third man came up behind Owens, police say, telling him to "shut up and keep walking."

Prosecutors say that man was Williams.

The man directed Owens into a back storage room, ordered him to lie face down and then shot him twice in the back at close range with a 12-gauge shotgun, according to prosecutors.

Accomplices and friends implicated Williams in the killing, saying he bragged about the shooting and imitated the noises Owens made as he died. Prosecutors said a shotgun shell found at the scene matched a gun purchased by Williams.

Rebecca Owens has been pushing for Williams' execution since she found out he was still alive. She says her father's life should be spotlighted rather than Williams'.

She has distant memories of her father, of him running on the beach, working on cars in the front yard, and laughing at her aversion to liver.

She has flown to California to visit his grave and to speak about the effect the crime had on her. She initiated a boycott of "Redemption," the film starring Jamie Foxx that tells the story of Williams' life. And she plans to be at San Quentin State Prison when Williams dies by lethal injection.

"I want it to be done, to see it over," she said.

Wayne Owens, Albert's brother, won't be watching outside the death chamber. He says he doesn't support capital punishment in most cases, and in fact would support clemency for Williams if he was guaranteed it wouldn't lead to freedom.

"If Williams would sign a contract saying he would drop his attempts at parole, I would support clemency," the 55-year-old Owens said in a telephone interview from his home outside Kansas City, Kansas. "If I could believe that he would spend the rest of his life in prison and continue the good works he is doing, I would be all for it.

"I hate the idea of the death penalty."

Albert Owens' murder was just the first that Williams committed, prosecutors say.

On March 11, 1979, 12 days after the 7-Eleven shooting, someone broke down the door that led to a private office at the Brookhaven Motel on South Vermont Avenue in Los Angeles. The sound woke Robert Yang in the room he shared with his wife. He heard his family screaming and then gunshots.

Yang found the body of his mother, Tsai-Shai Yang, 63. She had been hit by shotgun blasts in the abdomen and tailbone and died instantly.

Yang's father, Yen-I Yang, 76, and 43-year-old sister, Yee-Chen Lin, had been shot and were gasping for air. They died the next morning. Someone had stolen about $100 from the cash register.

Prosecutors say witnesses and a shell casing found at the scene proved that Williams committed the slayings. In a letter opposing clemency, the Los Angeles County district attorney called Williams a cold-blooded killer.

The Yang family believes the guilty verdict against Williams was just and opposes clemency, according to Attorney General Bill Lockyer's office.

Rebecca Owens is also convinced Williams is guilty. She can't reconcile his professed conversion to nonviolence with the brutality of the killings, and says his anti-gang efforts are meaningless without an apology for her father's death. Williams maintains that he didn't kill anybody and says he was convicted because of coerced and fabricated testimony from people seeking leniency for their crimes.

"He hasn't even confessed—how can he be a model?" Owens said. "If people choose not to go into crime after reading his work, that's because they choose it, not because of him.

"He refuses to take responsibility for his actions," she said. "His apology (for the gang lifestyle), give me a break. His victims are still faceless people. I don't want him dead because I think the death penalty will deter people from crime, but I do believe he should not be living on taxpayer money."

Albert Owens' stepmother, Lora Owens, wrote a letter to Schwarzenegger saying that Williams does not deserve clemency and that his professed redemption is an atrocity.

"To be redeemed, one must accept responsibility for the deeds and not claim to be redeemed to get out of the punishment set forth," Lora Owens wrote. "Williams has declared his own style of redemption for his own gain.

"He is a murderer and has caused the Owens family anguish for the last 26 years," she wrote. "His just punishment, his execution, could provide us some closure and peace."

Wayne Owens said his brother was in the midst of his own redemption when he was murdered.

He had problems in the Army and difficulty getting along with his family, so he moved to Southern California from the Midwest to try to straighten out his life. He had divorced his wife and found the 7-Eleven job, and was working to regain custody of his children.

He had lived in the Los Angeles County city of Pomona as a child and thought it would be a nice place to raise his own children, Wayne Owens said.

"He went out there and left everything behind in the hopes of starting over," his brother said. "He was living in a small room all by himself, with no friends. He had been through a divorce, lost custody, and had all kinds of family issues that were unresolved.

"He must have been so lonely."

MEASURE OF A MAN'S LIFE

Questions of redemption, atonement and clemency swirl as Stanley Tookie Williams' execution date approaches

As A Redeemer

By Leslie Fulbright, Chronicle Staff Writer

A .45-caliber bullet didn't lead Diego Garcia to give up the violent gang life he had known for years. Stanley Tookie Williams did.

Garcia, who grew up in the housing projects on Richmond's Easter Hill, joined a gang at age 9 and took part in drug deals, beatings and drive-by shootings before he was shot when he was 18. Months of recovery gave him plenty of time to think about making changes.

"I was completely confused. I didn't know whether I should choose the right path," said Garcia, now 30. "I read Tookie's books and it inspired me. I related to him. The books are different because it is the co-founder of the Crips giving you a message. Tookie caught my attention."

Williams is scheduled to be executed at San Quentin State Prison Dec. 13 for the shotgun murders of four people in the Los Angeles area in 1979. He maintains he is innocent, an assertion no court has agreed with, and now his lawyers are pinning their hopes on a clemency hearing Thursday before Gov. Arnold Schwarzenegger.

His attorneys and the high-profile figures who have been drawn to Williams' cause—including the Rev. Jesse Jackson, rapper Snoop Dogg and celebrities such as Jamie Foxx and Bianca Jagger—say Williams is worth more alive than dead. He has co-authored 10 books from Death Row laying out the evils of gangs, many of them directed at children, spoken by phone at anti-violence summits, and lent his name to an Internet peace project that links disadvantaged youths around the world.

"He is such a well-known member of the Crips that he is held in high esteem," said Alfonso Valdez, an investigator with the Orange County district attorney's office and expert on California gangs. "I have spoken to kids who consider him a demigod, a very high-ranking gang member. That means they listen to him."

Garcia, who now works with underprivileged students in Richmond, says he is living proof of Williams' ability to persuade gang members that the criminal life is not the way to go.

"Stanley changed my life," he said.

Those opposed to clemency say Williams should not be promoted as a role model, that he is an unrepentant criminal who should be executed for his crimes.

"His work doesn't mitigate the fact that he killed four people and started a gang that is still killing, dealing drugs and committing other crimes," said Jane Alexander, co-founder of Citizens Against Homicide, a Marin County support group for the families of homicide victims. "We want the execution to go on as planned."

"Measure of a Man's Life" by Leslie Fulbright from *San Francisco Chronicle*, December 4, 2005. Reprinted by permission of San Francisco Chronicle.

Crusade to Change Lives

Williams, 51, started his public crusade against violence in a hotel ballroom in 1993. He had already spent 12 years on Death Row after being convicted of murdering Albert Owens, a clerk at a Whittier (Los Angeles County) 7-Eleven store, in a February 1979 robbery, and the owners of a Los Angeles motel, Yen-I Yang and Tsai-Shai Yang, and their adult daughter, Yee-Chen Lin, during another robbery 12 days later.

Hundreds of gang members who had gathered in the Los Angeles ballroom for a peace summit called Hands Across Watts watched a videotape Williams had filmed in a San Quentin visiting room.

Williams admitted he had helped build the Crips, a vicious Los Angeles gang, and said he regretted having done so. He said he was going to spend the rest of his life trying to persuade other gang members to change.

"I told them I never thought I could change my life, that I thought I would be a Crip forever," Williams said last week during an interview at San Quentin. "But I developed common sense, wisdom and knowledge. I changed."

Tony Muhammad, a minister with the Nation of Islam, remembers that day.

"I saw tears rolling down those young people's eyes after they watched that video," he said. "It was deep. Many of us who are free can't affect the gang culture the way he does."

The gang members' reactions convinced many that Williams could help save lives, and his work in the following years convinced more. Supporters say his renunciation of violence and the "Tookie Speaks Out" and "Life in Prison" books he wrote from his 4-by-9-foot cell are deterring youth from entering gangs and entitle him to mercy.

Early Years in Prison

Williams' first decade at San Quentin scarcely hinted at the reform he and his followers say he has undergone. He spent six years in solitary confinement for bad behavior that included fighting with inmates and threatening to assault staff.

Williams says he spent his time in solitary reading the dictionary, studying philosophy, psychology and black history. He found God in "the hole," and considers himself a member of many religions. His first series of books was published in 1996, and the following year the www.tookie.com Web site was launched. In 1998, "Life in Prison," intended for teenagers, was published, and the Internet Project for Street Peace started in 2000. Williams' autobiography and a movie about his life, "Redemption," starring Foxx, were both released in 2004.

His supporters say thousands of children have been rescued thanks to Williams' books. It's a tough point to prove, however, at least by looking at crime rates.

George Tita, an assistant professor of criminology at UC Irvine who has done extensive research on homicide rates in Watts and surrounding areas, says there are no numbers showing that killings declined as a result of the numerous gang peace summits held since the early 1990s.

"The gang peace summits have not had an impact on the levels of violence in Los Angeles, but that doesn't mean they don't have great value," Tita said. As for Williams, he said, youths "look at him as a role model, not for the old Tookie Williams but the new one. His books and message are important for the community, but there is no statistical evidence to show that they have changed murder rates."

His backers insist they've seen the proof in those who read Williams' books.

"I can tell you what it is like, but I've never been in a gang," said Jorja Leap, an adjunct professor at UCLA who has researched gang intervention for 20 years. "He is a role model for people who are thinking about leaving the gang life. He has credibility because he lived that life. The books are a building block in their survival."

Books Reach Children

The books are used in a number of classrooms around the country and elsewhere. In the Chicago public school district, 25 campuses with at-risk students have created a class using Williams' autobiography as the curriculum.

To get that program started, Williams talked via telephone with Chicago principals, answered questions and gave them advice for handling kids involved with gangs. Then, more than 250 seventh- and eighth-grade boys with life circumstances similar to Williams' were picked for the program. Its facilitators, described as motivated and encouraging, use lesson plans and activities based on Williams' writings.

Carole Ward Allen, a professor in Laney College's black studies department, said she uses Williams' autobiography "because I like the fact that he has made a change. My goal is to keep kids in education and on the straight track.

"I am working with kids from the hip-hop generation," Allen said. "Tookie has an impact because he spans 35 years of gang life."

Language of the Street

Williams' "Tookie Speaks Out" series, aimed at elementary school children, uses street language and glossaries explaining words such as homeboy (friend or partner), mobbing (large numbers of kids pushing to get what they want) and enemy (someone who wants to hurt you).

Williams tells his young readers that the power that came with being in a gang ended up hurting him. He writes about how it feels to lose friends to gunfire, how he suffered from a gunshot wound to his leg, how guns don't prove you are tough. He talks about his first fight and the pressures that pushed him to join up with criminals.

"I grew up poor and wanted a lot of things that other kids had," Williams wrote. "Most of my homeboys were poor too. We would gang-bang to get what our parents couldn't afford to buy us. But now I know it's better to have less of the things you want than to get them by stealing, selling drugs or hurting others."

"Life in Prison," aimed at a high school audience, tells of the humiliation of being strip-searched in jail, the claustrophobia that comes with living in a cell and the violence of everyday prison life.

Jessie Muldoon, a teacher at Roosevelt Middle School in East Oakland, uses Williams' books, movie and Web site regularly for classroom discussions.

"The kids are now following the case on a day-to-day basis," she said. "They are interested because of the gang element. They are not necessarily in gangs, but know people who are.

"To know he has turned himself around from inside prison is not lost on them," Muldoon said. "They pass the books and newspaper articles around."

Writing Coach

Williams has authored nine of his books with Barbara Becnel. The two met in January 1993 when she was writing a story about Los Angeles gangs for *Essence* magazine. She says that at the time she thought he was guilty—she has since changed her mind—but the 1993 peace summit convinced her that his message was worth sharing.

"I was watching those kids and how they were entranced by him, and a lightbulb went off in my head," Becnel said. "I knew he could save lives. I got over my moral dilemma that day. I had an obligation, for my son and my grandson and all the African American males in my family."

Williams formed the Crips in 1970 with his friend Raymond Washington. He admits being involved with drugs and fighting, but not to the killings that sent him to San Quentin. He says he never imagined the gang would grow to its current size, and says that once the Crips moved from fists to guns, the violence spiraled out of control.

"As a result of Williams' actions, this gang is now active throughout the United States, as well as other countries across the globe," the Los Angeles County district attorney wrote in asking Schwarzenegger to deny Williams' request for clemency. "This gang is responsible for the regular commission of crimes such as murder, rape, robbery and drug sales."

Valdez, the gang expert, said Williams was one of the original members of the Crips and recruited others to the gang. However, he said, not all Crips fall under the same umbrella.

"Stanley helped start it and then it snowballed," Valdez said. "African American gangs decided to use the blue color, but were independent. Crips have always been a conglomeration of different sets or cliques that fly the blue color."

Williams said in his prison interview that "blaming me for all the gang activity is like blaming all white people for slavery or racial profiling. It is absurd to hold one man responsible."

Execution Draws Near

As Williams' execution date approaches, supporters' efforts to save him are growing more frantic. The NAACP plans a tour of California in the days before the clemency hearing. There are scheduled showings of "Redemption" and planned rallies in front of the governor's office. A round-the-clock vigil at the San Quentin gates will start today.

At least some of that interest has been stirred by the five Nobel Peace Prize nominations Williams has garnered since 2000. The first nomination was the work of Mario Fehr, a member of the Swiss Parliament and critic of the death penalty who says his goal in part was to get people talking about the case.

Those who are unimpressed by Williams note that any professor of social science, history, philosophy, law or theology can make a nomination for the prize. There are about 150 names submitted each year.

The nominations, along with his Internet project, have earned Williams worldwide recognition. He says he gets 20 to 30 letters a day from supporters and children who have read his work.

"I can't respond to them all," he said. "So I deal with the ones who are in pain and need immediate help. It's part of my redemption."

Messages from the Heart

Leadership program teaches self-confidence through public speaking

By Dwana Simone Bain

Independent Newspapers

BURLINGAME – A student poises himself at the podium to speak. Calmly and clearly, he tells the crowd of his experiences volunteering and mentoring at Washington Elementary School.

He speaks proudly of how his bilingual ability helped him work with the younger Spanish-speaking children. "I hope the kids got something out of it," he closes, "because I did."

On either side of the crowded room are the boy's own mentors in public speaking. English teacher Jim Burke and Toastmaster Elsie Robertson smile as they watch this sophomore delivering his final speech of the Youth Leadership Program, Toastmasters International.

Several teens stood up before a crowd of teachers and community members on a recent Friday afternoon, speaking with little shyness or hesitation.

It was tough to tell that only weeks earlier, many of them were nervous about public speaking.

"I'm so very proud of all of them because they've really come a long way", said Robertson, who coordinated the program. "The first speeches were quite painful—like going to the dentist—and now you can barely shut them up,"she said with a smile.

Guest speaker Dave Katz, a tutor with Ace Homework Help, offered the students a 10-step lesson on ambition. Among the tips, "Break through your fears," Katz said. "I have witnessed people in here that couldn't put three words together in a row, and now they're up at this podium doing extremely well."

This is the second year the leadership program—sponsored by the San Mateo Toastmasters Club 191 and facilitated by Robertson—has been held at Burlingame High School.

School to Career Site Coordinator Beth Pascal first explored the idea of Toastmasters on campus for a public speaking course. However, Pascal was told, the program works best with smaller groups.

"I started thinking about Jim (Burke's) class," she said. The 17 student Toastmasters are part of Burke's Access program, which is designed to help students live up to the potential they display. Burke selects students that show great potential, though their grades might not reflect their abilities.

The students largely run the leadership sessions, Pascal said. "It just empowers the kids because they're the ones who are in control of the day." The students elect a president and officers twice during the eight-week course.

During the course, students prepared at least two speeches each. They took turns evaluating each other's speeches for delivery, effectiveness of opening content, and closing. Students also participated in "table topics," speaking extemporaneously on selected subjects.

Each week, students voted for a "best speaker" and "best evaluator."

Abiding by Toastmasters guidelines, speeches and evaluations were carefully timed, with those exceeding the allowed time limit disqualified from winning. Each week the winners received a ribbon. Those who scored the most points in the course overall were awarded a special certificate at the course's culmination Dec. 13.

"It was interesting to watch the progression from the very first meeting with the students to the culmination of the program, and see the growth that occurred," Pascal said. "You could see how they felt more empowered and their self-esteem had really been affected."

Building the students' confidence was an important goal of the leadership course.

MySpace.com article
The siren call of myspace.com

Do you MySpace? A growing number of South Sound teens use the Web site to express themselves and meet friends, but some adults worry about their sharing personal information.

By DEBBY ABE

The News Tribune

Eighteen-year-old Aaron VanMeer's daily routine goes something like this: Get home from school, grab a snack and slide in front of the family computer for his daily fix.

He's just gotta log on to MySpace.com, the Web site where millions of teens and young adults gather to socialize.

For an hour - OK, maybe three or four sometimes - the Puyallup High School senior sends messages to some of the 149 friends listed on his site, tinkers with his site profile and surfs through other MySpace pages.

"This Web site is pretty important to me and my friends' social lives. . . . It's an unphysical way of hanging out," he said. "It's probably the first and last thing I do each and every night."

MySpace.com, along with similar sites, has exploded into a social necessity for more and more young people in the South Sound and across the country.

The free site allows members to create a personal Web page, called a profile, describing themselves and their interests.

Users can send e-mail and instant messages, and post music samples, snapshots and blogs by themselves and friends.

They can download music, talk to local and national band members, meet people and join online groups to ramble about topics as diverse as scrapbooking, music from the '90s or surviving cancer.

Yet for all the enthusiasm the site generates, it's also raising concerns among some parents and causing headaches for schools.

Parents wonder about the safety and content of the site, where tech-savvy kids spend hours each day communicating in the anonymity of cyberspace.

"The fact you don't know who you're meeting on there is kind of scary," said Bonney Lake resident Kim Halter, whose 14-year-old son recently joined MySpace. "It makes him happy, so I hate to just cut him off. I do watch him and limit the time he's on there."

Meanwhile, high schools are starting to see spillover effects from the site now that such a mass of teens has a forum to communicate with electronic speed.

"www.MySpace.com has hit schools with a vengeance," said Jim Boyce, dean of student affairs at White River High School in Buckley. "We have seen a very negative impact with MySpace.com as students from our school and others use it for negative purposes

such as threats, harassment and malicious gossip."

Massive popularity

Launched in January 2004, MySpace.com counts more than 46 million members. In November, an Internet measurement service found MySpace was the third-most-viewed site on the Internet in terms of total page views, outranking Google and eBay.

The site is open to anyone 14 or older, and advertisers use the site to reach 16- to 34-year-olds, according to information forwarded by Rena Grant with Edelman public relations firm for MySpace.

VanMeer, the high school senior, speculates most students at Puyallup High have a MySpace account. A quick search on the site found more than 900 users who say they attend the 1,650-student school.

Samantha Smith, a 15-year-old Curtis High School sophomore in University Place, says one of the most commonly asked questions when meeting another teen these days is "Do you have a MySpace?"

"Most of my friends at school are on it," she said.

If anything, users say one of the site's biggest downsides is too much MySpace.

"It pretty much is ruining my life because I'm constantly checking on it at work, at home, you name it," said Travis Noble, 19, a Pierce College student who estimates he spends up to six hours a day on the site. "It's such a time-waster. You spend your time on there instead of doing things you should be doing."

University of Washington sociology professor and author Pepper Schwartz sees MySpace and similar social networking sites as a means to connect people in new ways and to maintain less intense relationships across distance and time.

It also feeds peoples' desires to be a star.

"This allows you to be on the Web and to have your own page," she said. "People like to read about their friends, their hobbies. We're interested in ourselves and others."

MySpace pages are as unique as each individual. Some feature girls' dreams of the perfect date, photos of favorite actors and screen backgrounds decorated with hearts.

Others include photos of 16-year-olds mugging next to half-empty bottles of beer. Raunchier profiles ooze lewd and profane language and display snapshots of barely clothed women.

All sites contain thumbnail photos of virtual "friends" - MySpace users who've requested or been asked to join the member's friends list, enabling them to exchange e-mail and post messages on each others' sites.

Not all users are enamored with the site.

Travis Collett, 17, occasionally uses his MySpace account, but he said, "Most of the people in advanced placement classes (at Tacoma's Wilson High School) don't have them. A lot of them think it's ridiculous, it's an attention-getter. I think it's a teenage girl thing."

Schools, parents worry

Parent concerns have grown amid national media reports of problems at schools over information posted on MySpace sites or isolated cases of men assaulting or starting sexual relationships with underage girls they've met through the site.

In Graham, Claudia Chapman limits her 15-year-old daughter, Dani Clark, to chatting with known friends. Dani also must give Chapman her password, let her mom check her site profile and sit at the computer when the teen chats online.

"I've heard so much bad stuff about MySpace," Chapman said. "Predators . . . can come in and act like a high schooler. Unless we know who they are, there's blocked access to her. I don't want her to become a statistic."

Dani says her friends would flip out if their parents were as strict, but she doesn't mind.

"I understand my mom's trying to watch out for me," the Graham Kapowsin High sophomore said. "That's the one thing my mom and I can do, is play on the computer."

The Washington State Patrol's Missing and Exploited Children

Task Force began working on its first MySpace case a couple of weeks ago by posing as a teenager with a site, said Detective Sgt. Dan Sharp, who supervises the task force.

"We've noticed how the language and chatting in there is very sexual in nature," Sharp said. "Then we received a profile of an adult advertising himself as being over the age of 18, and his language was sexual in nature."

Preteens and adults alike should remember that personal information they post and discuss on MySpace can go to anyone on the Internet, including predators or pornographers, Sharp said.

He advises against placing a name, age, address, school, personal photo or other identifying information anywhere on the Web.

When a News Tribune reporter asked MySpace.com about safety concerns, the company's public relations firm referred to the site's safety tips area and provided a news release about its partnership with wiredsafety.org to create a safer site.

MySpace.com lists extensive safety tips, and the news release said the site has algorithms, specially designed software and staff to monitor the site for rule violators and underage users.

"If we find out a user is under 14, we will delete his or her profile," the safety tips say.

The list tells parents how to remove information from their child's site or delete the profile altogether. MySpace profiles also can be set so that users must approve who can view their site and send them e-mail.

Many teen users say they take care to avoid problems.

Jill Nguyen, an 18-year-old Foss High School senior, says she made up some of her profile details both as a joke and to keep from giving out too much personal information. She uses the site to communicate with friends, not meet new people.

"I don't think it's that dangerous," she said of MySpace, "but you should always be cautious."

Difficult to police

Aside from attracting predators, My Space, like any type of online communication, can lead to misunderstandings and become a technological monster.

Although most schools attempt to block the site from appearing on school computers, students often find ways to enter.

Mount Tahoma High commercial design teacher Lisa-Marie McDonald said students constantly try to sneak onto MySpace on one of the 30 computers in her room. Sometimes, they're successful.

If she catches them on the site twice, she bans them from her class computers for the rest of the quarter.

"It's the hugest problem I have," McDonald said.

Meanwhile, at White River High, administrators have intervened to prevent disagreements over what's written on MySpace blogs from

escalating into something serious, said Boyce, the dean of student affairs.

"Put yourself in a teenager's shoes. Someone writes in and says 'Jim Boyce is blah blah blah.' You'd write in and say 'no he isn't.' Another person would say 'you shut up.' That would happen at a school in the course of a day, but it doesn't have the speed of the Internet."

At Curtis High in University Place, administrators have asked students to remove two inappropriate photos posted on MySpace profiles in the past year, said associate principal David Hammond.

In one case, three cheerleaders wearing their Curtis outfits were photographed playfully spanking the backside of a fourth uniformed cheerleader, who was bent over to receive the swats.

In the other case, a boy took a camera-phone photo of a teacher, and posted the picture and inappropriate comments about the teacher on his MySpace site, Hammond said.

While schools generally can't dictate what content students put on personal sites outside school, Hammond said they can impose discipline if the content leads to threats or violence at school.

With the less-serious Curtis cases, administrators talked with the students and their parents, and the students voluntarily removed the photos, he said.

Despite the concerns about MySpace and similar sites, neither the school administrators nor

Detective Sharp suggest banning teens from using MySpace.

Instead, they say young users need to learn about Internet hazards and parents need to monitor their computer use.

"I'm confident with some education, kids will do just fine," Boyce said. "It's up to parents and educators to help them become aware."

Robo-Legs

New prosthetic limbs are providing increased mobility for many amputees—and blurring the line between humans and machines

By Michael Marriott

With his blond hair, buff torso, and megawatt smile, Cameron Clapp is in many ways the quintessential California teenager. There are, however, a few things that set him apart: For starters, this former skater boy is now making his way through life on a pair of shiny, state-of-the-art robotic legs.

"I make it look easy," he says.

Clapp, 19, lost both his legs above the knee and his right arm just short of his shoulder after getting hit by a train almost five years ago near his home in Grover Beach, Calif. Following years of rehabilitation and a series of prosthetics, each more technologically advanced than the last, he has become part of a new generation of people who are embracing breakthrough technologies as a means of overcoming their own bodies' limitations.

"I do have a lot of motivation and self-esteem," Clapp says, "but I might look at myself differently if technology was not on my side."

The technology he's referring to is the C-Leg. Introduced by Otto Bock HealthCare, a German company that makes advanced prosthetics, the C-Leg combines computer technology with hydraulics. Sensors monitor how the leg is being placed on terrain and microprocessors guide the limb's hydraulic system, enabling it to simulate a natural step. It literally does the walking for the walker. The technology, however, is not cheap; a single C-Leg can cost more than $40,000.

The C-Leg is one of the examples of how blazing advancements, including tiny programmable microprocessors, lightweight composite materials, and keener sensors, are restoring remarkable degrees of mobility to amputees, says William Hanson, president of Liberating Technologies Inc., a Massachusetts company that specializes in developing and distributing advanced prosthetic arms and hands.

Three Sets of Legs

For example, Clapp, who remains very involved in athletics despite his condition, has three different sets of specialized prosthetic legs: one for walking, one for running, and one for swimming. In June, he put all of them to use at the Endeavor Games in Edmond, Okla.—an annual sporting event for athletes with disabilities—where he competed in events like the 200-meter dash and the 50-yard freestyle swim.

Man or Machine?

But increased mobility is only part of the story. Something more subtle, and possibly far-reaching, is also occurring: The line that has long separated human beings from the machines that assist them is blurring, as complex technologies become a visible part of the people who depend upon them.

Increasingly, amputees, especially young men like Clapp, and soldiers who have lost limbs in Afghanistan and Iraq, are choosing not to hide their prosthetics under clothing as previous generations did. Instead, some of the estimated 1.2 million amputees in the United States—more than two thirds of whom are men—proudly polish and decorate their electronic limbs for all to see.

Long an eerie theme in popular science fiction, the integration of humans with machines has often been presented as a harbinger of a soulless future, populated with flesh-and-metal cyborgs like RoboCops and

Robo-Legs" by Michael Marriott from *The New York Times*, June 20, 2005. © 2005 The New York Times Co. Reprinted by permission.

Terminators. But now major universities like Carnegie Mellon and the University of California at Berkeley, as well as private companies and the U.S. military, are all exploring ways in which people can be enhanced by strapping themselves into wearable robotics.

"There is a kind of cyborg consciousness, a fluidity at the boundaries of what is flesh and what is machine, that has happened behind our backs," says Sherry Turkle, director of the Initiative on Technology and Self at the Massachusetts Institute of Technology, which studies technology's impact on humanity. "The notion that your leg is a machine part and it is exposed, that it is an enhancement, is becoming comfortable in the sense that it can be made a part of you."

While some users are eager to display their prosthetic marvels, others like them to appear more human. Besides selling prosthetics, Liberating Technologies, for one, offers 19 kinds of silicone sleeves for artificial limbs to make them seem more natural.

"There are two things that are important; one is functionality and the other is cosmetic," says Hanson, the company's president. "Various people weigh those differences differently. There are trade-offs."

But many young people, especially those who have been using personal electronics since childhood, are comfortable recharging their limbs' batteries in public and plugging their prosthetics into their computers to adjust the software, Hanson says.

Nick Springer, 20, a student at Eckerd College in St. Petersburg, Fla., who lost his arms and legs to meningitis when he was 14, recalls doing just that at a party when the lithium-ion batteries for his legs went dead.

"I usually get 30 hours out of them before I have to charge them again," he says. "But I didn't charge them up the day before."

Terminator Legs

When his legs ran out of power, he spent most of his time sitting on a couch talking to people while his legs were plugged into an electrical outlet nearby. According to Springer, no one at the party seemed to care, and his faith in his high-tech appendages appears unfazed. "I love my Terminator legs," he says.

Springer also remembers going to see Star Wars: Episode III—Revenge of the Sith with his father. While he liked the movie, he found the final scenes—in which Anakin Skywalker loses his arms and legs in a light-saber battle and is rebuilt with fully functional prosthetics to become the infamous Darth Vader—a little far-fetched.

"We have a long way to go before we get anything like that," he says. "But look how far humanity has come in the past decade. Who knows? The hardest part is getting the ball rolling. We pretty much got it rolling."

The Second Coming

W.B. Yeats

TURNING and turning in the widening gyre
The falcon cannot hear the falconer;
Things fall apart; the centre cannot hold;
Mere anarchy is loosed upon the world,
The blood-dimmed tide is loosed, and everywhere
The ceremony of innocence is drowned;
The best lack all conviction, while the worst
Are full of passionate intensity.

Surely some revelation is at hand;
Surely the Second Coming is at hand.
The Second Coming! Hardly are those words out
When a vast image out of Spiritus Mundi
Troubles my sight: somewhere in sands of the desert
A shape with lion body and the head of a man,
A gaze blank and pitiless as the sun,
Is moving its slow thighs, while all about it
Reel shadows of the indignant desert birds.
The darkness drops again; but now I know
That twenty centuries of stony sleep
Were vexed to nightmare by a rocking cradle,
And what rough beast, its hour come round at last,
Slouches towards Bethlehem to be born?

"The Second Coming" reprinted with the permission of Scribner, an imprint of Simon & Schuster Adult Publishing Group, from *The Collected Works of W.B. Yeats: Volume I: The Poems, Revised* by Richard J. Finneran. © 1983, © 1989 by Anne Yeats. © 1924 by Macmillan Company, renewed by Bertha Georgie Yeats.

Sonnet 18
William Shakespeare

Shall I compare thee to a summer's day?

Thou art more lovely and more temperate:

Rough winds do shake the darling buds of May,

And summer's lease hath all too short a date;

Sometime too hot the eye of heaven shines,

And often is his gold complexion dimmed;

And every fair from fair sometime declines,

By chance, or nature's changing course untrimmed:

But thy eternal summer shall not fade,

Nor lose possession of that fair thou ow'st,

Nor shall death brag thou wand'rest in his shade,

When in eternal lines to time thou grow'st.

    So long as men can breathe, or eyes can see,

    So long lives this, and this gives life to thee.

Sonnet 116
William Shakespeare

Let me not to the marriage of true minds

Admit impediments. Love is not love

Which alters when it alteration finds,

Or bends with the remover to remove.

O no! it is an ever-fix'd mark

That looks on tempests and is never shaken;

It is the star to every wandering bark,

Whose worth's unknown, although his height be taken.

Love's not Time's fool, though rosy lips and cheeks

Within his bending sickle's compass come.

Love alters not with his brief hours and weeks,

But bears it out even to the edge of doom.

    If this be error and upon me proved,

    I never writ, nor no man ever loved.

Time 100: Bruce Lee

With nothing but his hands, feet and a lot of attitude, he turned the little guy into a tough guy.

By JOEL STEIN

Monday, June 14, 1999

Not a good century for the Chinese. After dominating much of the past two millenniums in science and philosophy, they've spent the past 100 years being invaded, split apart and patronizingly lectured by the West. And, let's face it, this communism thing isn't working out either.

But in 1959 a short, skinny, bespectacled 18-year-old kid from Hong Kong traveled to America and declared himself to be John Wayne, James Dean, Charles Atlas and the guy who kicked your butt in junior high. In an America where the Chinese were still stereotyped as meek house servants and railroad workers, Bruce Lee was all steely sinew, threatening stare and cocky, pointed finger—a Clark Kent who didn't need to change outfits. He was the redeemer, not only for the Chinese but for all the geeks and dorks and pimpled teenage masses that washed up at the theaters to see his action movies. He was David, with spin-kicks and flying leaps more captivating than any slingshot.

He is the patron saint of the cult of the body: the almost mystical belief that we have the power to overcome adversity if only we submit to the right combinations of exercise, diet, meditation and weight training; that by force of will, we can sculpt ourselves into demigods. The century began with a crazy burst of that philosophy. In 1900 the Boxer rebels of China who attacked the Western embassies in Beijing thought that martial-arts training made them immune to bullets. It didn't. But a related fanaticism—on this side of sanity—exists today: the belief that the body can be primed for killer perfection and immortal endurance.

Lee never looked like Arnold Schwarzenegger or achieved immortality. He died at 32 under a cloud of controversy, in his mistress's home, of a brain edema, which an autopsy said was caused by a strange reaction to a prescription painkiller called Equagesic. At that point, he had starred in only three released movies, one of which was unwatchably bad, the other two of which were watchably bad. Although he was a popular movie star in Asia, his *New York Times* obit ran only eight sentences, one of which read "Vincent Canby, the film critic of the *New York Times*, said that movies like *Fists of Fury* make 'the worst Italian western look like the most solemn and noble achievements of the early Soviet Cinema.'"

What Canby missed is that it's the moments between the plot points that are worth watching. It was the ballet of precision violence that flew off the screen; every combination you can create in *Mortal Kombat* can be found in a Lee movie. And even with all the special-effects money that went into *The Matrix*, no one could make violence as beautiful as Lee's. He had a cockiness that passed for charisma. And when he whooped like a crane, jumped in the air and simultaneously kicked two bad guys into unconsciousness, all while punching out two others mostly offscreen, you knew the real Lee could do that too.

He spent his life turning his small body into a large weapon. Born sickly in a San Francisco hospital (his father, a Hong Kong opera singer, was on tour there), he would be burdened with two stigmas that don't become an action hero: an undescended testicle and a female name, Li Jun Fan, which his mother gave him to ward off the evil spirits out to snatch valuable male children. She even pierced one of his ears, because evil spirits always fall for the pierced-ear trick. Lee quickly became obsessed with martial arts and body building and not much else. As a child actor back in Hong Kong, Lee appeared in 20 movies and rarely in school. He was part of a small gang that was big enough to cause his mother to ship him to America before his 18th birthday so he could claim his dual-citizenship and avoid winding up in jail.

"Bruce Lee: with nothing but his hands" by Joel Stein from *Time*, July 14, 1999. © 1999 Time Inc. Reprinted by permission.

Boarding at a family friend's Chinese restaurant in Seattle, Lee got a job teaching the Wing Chun style of martial arts that he had learned in Hong Kong. In 1964, at a tournament in Long Beach, Calif.—the first major American demonstration of kung fu—Lee, an unknown, ripped through black belt Dan Inosanto so quickly that Inosanto asked to be his student.

Shortly after, Lee landed his first U.S. show-biz role: Kato in *The Green Hornet*, a 1966-67 TV superhero drama from the creators of *Batman*. With this minor celebrity, he attracted students like Steve McQueen, James Coburn and Kareem Abdul-Jabbar to a martial art he called Jeet Kune Do, "the way of the intercepting fist." Living in L.A., he became the vanguard on all things '70s. He was a physical-fitness freak: running, lifting weights and experimenting with isometrics and electrical impulses meant to stimulate his muscles while he slept. He took vitamins, ginseng, royal jelly, steroids and even liquid steaks. A rebel, he flouted the Boxer-era tradition of not teaching kung fu to Westerners even as he hippily railed against the robotic exercises of other martial arts that prevented self-expressive violence. One of his admonitions: "Research your own experiences for the truth. Absorb what is useful. Add what is specifically your own. The creating individual . . . is more important than any style or system." When he died, doctors found traces of marijuana in his body. They could have saved some money on the autopsy and just read those words.

Despite his readiness to embrace American individuality and culture, Lee couldn't get Hollywood to embrace him, so he returned to Hong Kong to make films. In these films, Lee chose to represent the little guy, though he was a very cocky little guy. And so, in his movies, he'd fight for the Chinese against the invading Japanese or the small-town family against the city-living drug dealers. There were, for some

reason, usually about 100 of these enemies, but they mostly died as soon as he punched them in the face. The plots were uniform: Lee makes a vow not to fight; people close to Lee are exploited and killed; Lee kills lots of people in retaliation; Lee turns himself in for punishment.

The films set box-office records in Asia, and so Hollywood finally gave him the American action movie he longed to make. But Lee died a month before the release of his first U.S. film, *Enter the Dragon*. The movie would make more than $200 million, and college kids would pin Lee posters next to Che Guevara's. In the end, Lee could only exist young and in the movies. Briefly, he burst out against greater powers before giving himself over to the authorities. A star turn in a century not good for the Chinese.

Joel Stein is a columnist and staff writer for TIME *magazine.*

Vocation
William Stafford

This dream the world is having about itself
includes a trace on the plains of the Oregon trail,
a groove in the grass my father showed us all
one day while meadowlarks were trying to tell
something better about to happen.

I dreamed the trace to the mountains, over the hills,
and there a girl who belonged wherever she was.
But then my mother called us back to the car:
she was afraid; she always blamed the place,
the time, anything my father planned.

Now both of my parents, the long line through the plain,
the meadowlarks, the sky, the world's whole dream
remain, and I hear him say while I stand between the
two, helpless, both of them part of me:
"Your job is to find what the world is trying to be."

"Vocation" by William Stafford. Copyright 1962, 1998 by the Estate of William Stafford. Reprinted from *The Way It Is: New & Selected Poems* with the permission of Graywolf Press, Saint Paul, Minnesota.

WALKING OFF THE FAT, ACROSS THE LAND

At 400 Pounds, a Californian Set Off for New York. In Arizona, He's at 350.

By *Amy Argetsinger*
Washington Post Staff Writer

Friday, July 8, 2005; Page A03

PEACH SPRINGS, Ariz.

This week, his 13th on the road, has been the hardest thus far for Steve Vaught, a 400-pound man trying to walk across America.

On Sunday morning, he found a creek just as the desert heat forced a midday break. But when he woke from a nap and tried to fill his water bottles, the stream had already gone dry. Late that night, he walked right past his scheduled motel stop in Truxton, a flyspeck on historic Route 66 so slight it vanished when the sun went down.

On Monday, out of water in 102-degree heat and miles from any town, he sent a frantic text message to his wife, who called the local police. They drove him to a hotel, where he rested a night and a day, sick with dehydration. On Wednesday he started late and tangled with a scary dude on the desolate highway.

"I'm quitting," he told his wife this week. She said okay.

But within hours he hit the road again, as they always sort of knew he would. For quitting is not so easy when you're 500 miles from home.

This spring, as he neared his 40th birthday, Vaught had an epiphany: If he didn't lose the weight, he would die before 50. But dieting would not work, he decided, and neither would normal

exercise. He knew he was the kind of guy who could rationalize his way out of one three-mile walk after another. "My weakness," he said, "is the easy way out."

So Vaught made it hard. On April 10, he left his home in San Diego—and his wife and two children—and started walking, alone, to New York.

There's something about this nation's geography that inspires this kind of journey—to hike the Appalachian Trail, to kayak the entire Mississippi River, or just to drive from Maine to Key West, and maybe make sense of things along the way. Which is how it has gone for Vaught, on the road mulling issues far beyond weight or willpower. The trip has not gone completely as planned. He has only rarely come even close to the pace of 20 miles a day he estimated would put him in verdant Missouri by now, not Arizona in July.

He strained a couple of ligaments shortly after he started, and he lost three toenails climbing the final mountain pass out of California.

If he is very lucky, Vaught will clear 80 miles this week, a fraction of his 3,000-mile goal. On Wednesday, he remained deeply concerned about his ability to cover a 25-mile stretch of uninhabited desert between Seligman and Ash Fork.

On the bright side: That 400-pound man now weighs only 350.

HEALTH IMPLICATIONS

"Does this seem insane?" Vaught wants to know. He is a big guy, 6-foot-1, a former Marine and long-time tow-truck operator who, as the fat melts away from his cheekbones

and jaws, is beginning to bear a slight resemblance to the buffed-up actor Jerry O'Connell, but with a lumberjack beard and shock of hair like an unmowed lawn.

Well, that depends on what you mean by "insane." Doctors, certainly, would call it inadvisable. A seriously overweight person who embarks on any kind of strenuous physical activity could place dangerous stresses on his joints and heart, said Samuel Klein, director of the Center for Human Nutrition at Washington University in St. Louis.

And such activity is especially worrisome in an area of environmental extremes, without someone to support him, Klein said. Even if he weighed 100 pounds, "walking across a desert without someone standing next to him with an umbrella and a fan and Gatorade might really be a problem."

Vaught, meanwhile, has been almost completely on his own. For the first few days after he set off from the Pacific Ocean, his wife, April, would pick him at up the end of the day to bring him home to sleep at her mother's house, where the family is staying. Soon, though, he had gone far enough that he had to start camping; now he has not seen his family in three weeks.

Now and then a friend catches up with him for a few hours or days. But mostly it is just him and his 75-pound pack and the left-hand shoulder of the road.

Since he entered the desert, he has had to cut back his walking hours dramatically. Now he walks from about 5:30 to 8:30 in the morning, when he has to stop and find shelter—preferably in a store or post office if one is

"At 400 Pounds, a Californian Set Off for New York. In Arizona, he's at 350" by Amy Argetsinger from *Washington Post*, July 8, 2005, p. A03. © 2005, The Washington Post, reprinted with permission.

around, but usually under a bridge or in a culvert or bush.

He will sit there for 11 or 12 hours, until it is cool enough to walk again for a few hours. Just sit there. "I'm too bored to read," he says, or even take in the landscape more than he already has.

"It's beautiful for the first hour or so," he said. "And then it loses its impact."

Yet on the question of "insane," the responses to the Web site chronicling his journey—http://www.thefatmanwalking.com/—appear to be running heavily against. On a recent afternoon, Vaught accepts a ride from a reporter 35 miles down the road to a public library, where he checks his e-mail.

There is one from a 37-year-old guy preparing to run his first marathon. A 62-year-old woman planning to hike the Pacific Crest Trail. People in such places as St. Louis and Altoona, Pa., offering food and water and a place to stay when he comes their way. Over-weight people across the country begging to know Vaught's daily mileage so they can match it at home.

Only a few call him crazy. Almost all say what an inspiration he is.

It is something to think about, on those lonely and terrible days on the road, he says. "Now I have all these people not to let down."

Even at 400 pounds, he never thought of himself as a fat guy. Perhaps because he never used to be, perhaps because it was the least of his problems.

Fifteen years ago, he was the fun guy. A slew of girlfriends, a bunch of friends, a witty streak so hot he

would gladly take the stage at a comedy club open-mike night. Then one evening in October 1990, driving too fast against the setting sun, he struck and killed an elderly couple crossing the street.

The accident sent him to jail for 10 days, ruined him financially and dulled him emotionally. When he started to put on the weight, he just didn't care. He remembers little about the next three years.

After the birth of their first child, he grudgingly went to therapy, just so April would know she had done everything she could in case he killed himself. Medication snapped him out of his depression. But life didn't get any easier. A few businesses failed, and they went deep in debt on a house. And the weight, he realized, was bringing him down.

"There's nothing appealing about fat people," he says bluntly. "You can't impress them when you're fat." His jobs steadily declined in quality. In March he said he walked away from the latest, managing a muffler repair shop, after the owners sniped about him sitting down too much at work.

One morning that week, he turned to April in bed. "I ought to walk across the U.S.," he said. Once he left, he added, it would be hard for him to quit.

"If that's what it's going to take," she replied.

So he has a lot to think about as he walks. About the anger he carried around so long, and how pointless it seems now. About how accepting help from people doesn't shame him anymore, now that he sometimes has to ask strangers for

water. And about the value of living in the moment, of just surviving that next stretch of road.

"It has nothing to do with weight anymore," he says. "It's about getting back to the person I was."

Vaught gets the reporter to drive him back west to the outskirts of Peach Springs, near where he stopped walking. At 5 p.m., it's still 92 degrees, and he looks for a place in the shade where he can wait.

He sees it about 50 yards off the highway, a culvert over a now-abandoned part of the original Route 66. "This is good," he says. He lifts his pack onto his shoulders. The strap holding it to his still-massive gut now has eight inches of excess past the buckle, compared with two inches when he began.

He manages to heave his body over the guardrail and starts walking. By the time the car has turned around and driven past again, his 350 pounds have vanished into the desert.

Staff writer Catharine Skipp contributed to this report.

What Work Is
Phillip Levine

We stand in the rain in a long line
waiting at Ford Highland Park. For work.
You know what work is—if you're
old enough to read this you know what work
is, although you may not do it.
Forget you. This is about waiting,
shifting from one foot to another.
Feeling the light rain falling like mist
into your hair, blurring your vision
until you think you see your own brother
ahead of you, maybe ten places.
You rub your glasses with your fingers,
and of course it's someone else's brother,
narrower across the shoulders than
yours but with the same sad slouch, the grin
that does not hide the stubbornness,
the sad refusal to give in to
rain, to the hours wasted waiting,
to the knowledge that somewhere ahead
a man is waiting who will say, "No,
we're not hiring today," for any
reason he wants. You love your brother,
now suddenly you can hardly stand
the love flooding you for your brother,
who's not beside you or behind or
ahead because he's home trying to
sleep off a miserable night shift
at Cadillac so he can get up
before noon to study his German.
Works eight hours a night so he can sing
Wagner, the opera you hate most,
the worst music ever invented.
How long has it been since you told him
you loved him, held his wide shoulders,
opened your eyes wide and said those words,
and maybe kissed his cheek? You've never
done something so simple, so obvious,
not because you're too young or too dumb,
not because you're jealous or even mean
or incapable of crying in
the presence of another man, no,
just because you don't know what work is.

"What Work Is" from *What Work Is* by Philip Levine, © 1992 by Philip Levine. Used by permission of Alfred A. Knopf, a division of Random House, Inc.